Software
and
Intellectual Property
Protection

Software and Intellectual Property Protection

Copyright and Patent Issues
for Computer and Legal Professionals

BERNARD A. GALLER

Foreword by Jack E. Brown

QUORUM BOOKS
Westport, Connecticut • London

Library of Congress Cataloging-in-Publication Data

Galler, Bernard A.
    Software and intellectual property protection : copyright and patent
issues for computer and legal professionals / Bernard A. Galler ; foreword
by Jack E. Brown.
        p.   cm.
    Includes bibliographical references and index.
    ISBN 0–89930–974–7 (alk. paper)
    1. Software protection—Law and legislation—United States.
2. Copyright—Computer programs—United States. I. Title
KF3024.C6G35   1995
346.7304'82—dc20   94–40353
[347.306482]

British Library Cataloguing in Publication Data is available.

Library of Congress Catalog Card Number: 94–40353
ISBN: 0–89930–974–7

First published in 1995

Quorum Books, 88 Post Road West, Westport, CT 06881
An imprint of Greenwood Publishing Group, Inc.

Printed in the United States of America

The paper used in this book complies with the
Permanent Paper Standard issued by the National
Information Standards Organization (Z39.48–1984).

10 9 8 7 6 5 4 3 2 1

Contents

Foreword by Jack E. Brown   vii

Preface   ix

Acknowledgments   xi

Introduction   1

1 Legal Issues   7

2 Idea or Expression?   11

3 Software Patents   29

4 The Tangible Medium   47

5 Validity and Scope   55

6 Infringement   67

7 Substantial Similarity   77

8 Look and Feel   91

9 Reverse Engineering   105

10   The Clean Room Approach   125

11   Where Are We Now?   133

Appendixes
     A. A Review of the Fundamentals of Computer Technology   141
     B. An Example of a Patent   179
     C. A Concurring Opinion in *In re Alappat*   191
     D. Citations List   195
Recommended Reading   199
Index   201

Foreword

Jack E. Brown

Bernard Galler's book, *Software and Intellectual Property Protection*, is an exemplary reminder of what a master teacher can accomplish. Galler has produced a clear and near-comprehensive introduction to the issues that have arisen relating to the protection of computer software in the last two decades. He has done so through a lucid description, explanation, and brief discussion of about 30 featured copyright and patent cases, accompanied by a brilliant essay on the fundamentals of computer technology.

Galler played a part as an expert witness or advisor in some of the cases included in his text. That personal experience has informed his commentary and gives it an immediacy that makes it far more interesting than the heavier stuff found in legal tomes. In no instance has he given less than a fair, neutral account of the holding of a case.

The chapters on computer technology, however, are the real treasure. Every lawyer, judge, and lay person who seeks to comprehend the legal issues bearing on the protection of computer software would do well to start with Galler's exposition of the subject.

From his explanation of the codes of 0s and 1s, the formatting of instructions, and the history of computer languages through the function of operating system programs and the writing and processing of application programs, the reader is led from the seemingly simple to the obviously complex in a seamless style yielding constant illumination.

Galler's book is proof that the power of clear statement is the ultimate gift of the great teacher.

Preface

The modern history of electronic computers only spans about 45 years. In the last 25 years alone we have watched the software industry become one of the largest in the industrial world. All of the growing pains that more mature industries have lived through have been compressed for this industry into little more than one generation.

Part of these growing pains has been the confusion about the value of software as an asset and its protection from illegal copying and sale. In recent decades the U.S. Copyright Office and the U.S. Patent & Trademark Office have vacillated between providing protection for new writings and inventions and not allowing protection. Ultimately, Congress and the courts must sort out the various interests, taking into consideration the writers, inventors, and end users as well as the growing software industry and society itself.

A body of law evolves over centuries, first through laws passed by Congress (based on the Constitution) and then through the clarifications that result from specific precedent-setting cases. After a while, Congress reviews the situation and revises the laws, while attempting to take cognizance of new technologies that were not even anticipated when the law was last revised. Then the litigation starts again.

That is the situation with the very recent and rapid diffusion of computers throughout our society. The U.S. laws to protect intellectual property are as old as the Constitution, but the Founding Fathers could not have foreseen computers or software. Congress has tried, as we shall see, to adapt the intellectual property laws to accommodate new technologies such as the computer, television, videotapes, movies, and so on. But the computer introduces new problems that seem to some people to be unique. Can existing laws adequately and fairly apply to the new information age? What in fact has been happening?

This book is intended for several audiences: lawyers, computer professionals, and anyone interested in Intellectual Property Law as it applies to computer software. For all of these audiences, this book has been intended to make the underlying ideas as accessible as possible. Appendix A describes those aspects of computers that are most relevant to intellectual property law concerning computer software. Those who understand the world of computers may want to just skim this appendix, but anyone who is not comfortable with the technology should read it first as background support for the legal issues. The main part of the book reviews software copyright and patent issues as they have developed, through the opinions that the courts have written over the years. Of course, there is another body of law that applies to intellectual property, that is, trade secret law. There is little in that area that is peculiar to the computer, however, and I shall not develop that aspect here.

I am a computer scientist, not a lawyer. Fortunately, I have had a unique opportunity to participate as an expert witness in a number of the major cases involving computers and intellectual property. These include *NEC, Inc.* v. *Intel, Inc.*; *Lotus Development Corporation, Inc.* v. *Paperback Software International, Inc.*; *Apple Computer Corporation, Inc.* v. *Microsoft, Inc.*; and others. As a result, I have had to learn a great deal about copyright and patent protection and about legal procedures. The more I learned, the more I became convinced that it was important to share my insight with others who may be just as confused as I was initially about intellectual property laws and legal procedures and how they affect the computer software industry. That is why this book was written.

Acknowledgments

I express my appreciation to the many attorneys who have taught me so much. My special thanks go to Tom Barr, Jack Brown, Evan Chesler, Anthony Clapes, Robert Fischer, Hank Guttman, Kerry Konrad, Susan Kornfield, Bob Mullen, Bob Nolan, Paul Saunders, and Greg Stobbs.

Because of the multiple audiences mentioned in the Preface, I have had all or part of the manuscript reviewed by a number of professionals in the field, both lawyers involved with intellectual property and computer-knowledgeable people. As expected, they came back with quite different suggestions for improvement, most of which were incorporated. These reviewers were Silva Alpert, Jack E. Brown, Anthony Clapes, Aaron Finerman, Robert Fischer, Bruce Galler, Susan Kornfield, John Sayler, and Greg Stobbs. For their criticism, I am extremely grateful.

I express my appreciation to my wife, Enid Galler, for her support over the years, and especially during the writing of this book.

Software
and
Intellectual Property
Protection

Introduction

The ballet was about to start, and there was the usual bustle as the people in the audience found their seats and talked with friends. A group of students raced up the stairs to the highest balcony, which was all they could afford, and excitedly took their seats just as the curtain was about to go up. Their teacher was conducting the orchestra, and he had composed the music for this opening night of a new ballet.

The music started, the curtain rose, and the dance began. The audience was quiet now, but one could sense some agitation in the group of students in the top balcony. After a few moments, one of the students worked his way to the aisle, ran up the steps, burst through the exit door, and raced down three flights to the office of the ballet manager.

"He stole my music!" the student cried. There was a mixture of pride and anguish in his voice, but mostly pain. His music was being presented under someone else's name. His creation was no longer his, and no one would ever understand that it was he who had had that flash of inspiration, that exhilarating, frantic time when he could not write it all down quickly enough to capture the sounds that sang through his imagination. Someone who had not had that experience — perhaps was not capable of it — was taking credit for his creation.

The ballet manager could tell what was going through the student's mind. This was not the first time that he was hearing cries of plagiarism.

"I understand how you feel, young man. But you should consider this. How must your teacher feel if he has to take your music as his own?"[1]

The story is not new, only the details. Some people create, others copy. Why do people copy what they have not themselves created? Some copying is perfectly legitimate. In fact, most of us often borrow ideas, quotes, facts, and other writings that are in the public domain during our normal course of work. The kind of copying we are primarily concerned with here occurs when someone makes an exact copy of an original work of authorship without permission, or otherwise violates the various laws that have evolved in the area.

More specifically, this book focuses on the application of the copyright and patent laws in the computer software area, and the evolution of those laws as they have been applied to software. This is accomplished through an analysis of the issues involved, together with the various court decisions that have been necessary to clarify the laws. This clarification has been necessary because the specific nature of computer software and how it differs from other technologies was not always anticipated.

There is another kind of intellectual property protection called trade secret law. This depends on contractual arrangements with employees and customers regarding non-disclosure of proprietary information, and an aggressive effort is required to keep the information secret. Because computer software appears to fit rather well under existing law in this area, I shall not consider trade secret protection in this book.

There is an entire spectrum of possible ways to use information derived from the work of others. At one end is the explicit copying of actual text without any attribution, permission, or exemption from the Copyright Act. At the other end is permissible use of someone else's idea, according to the laws and norms of our society. Most of what we do lies somewhere in between, and the issues are complex.

Why would someone violate the copyright laws? Sometimes it is done for private gain. Perhaps this person finds himself under great pressure to produce something because his company's marketing people have already advertised a product, and he cannot deliver it on time, or a competitor's product is so successful he believes that his must be completely compatible with it. Whatever the reason, illegal copying happens with unfortunate frequency, and society long ago began to act to protect authors and inventors from the copiers.

Actually, copyright laws in Britain, from which our U.S. versions descended, were not originally intended to protect authors. There is evidence that these laws were enacted to give a non-terminating monopoly to printers and publishers, and to help the British government control what was available to the public to read (Patterson 1991). That was several hundred years ago. Later, as part of a move to break that monopoly, the justification was changed to protecting authors, but with a limited period of protection, and some important exemptions under the "fair use" provisions. These limitations to the authors' rights made sure that the public eventually did have access to their writings.

In the United States, this view of limited intellectual property protection was written into the United States Constitution, in Article 1, Section 8: "Congress shall have the power. . . . To promote the Progress of Science and useful Arts, by securing for limited Times to Authors and Inventors the exclusive Right to their respective Writings and Discoveries."

The most comprehensive protection legislation in this area was the Copyright Act of 1976; amendments in 1980 brought the original act more in line with advances in technology. This legislation reflects a view that our society needs creative people, and it needs to reward their contributions. At the same time, it codified some exemptions as "fair use" to guarantee the access of the public under certain conditions.

With regard to rewarding authors, the reasoning is that if there is no economic compensation, these creators might not be able to continue to participate in this way to improve our world. If others are allowed to copy their work, they may stop creating altogether. We would all lose.

On the other hand, if we discourage others from creating something new because they might be challenged as possibly copying someone else's work, then too often the world would be deprived of their accomplishments. As expressed in one legal opinion: "the purpose of the copyright law is to create the most efficient and productive balance between protection (incentive) and dissemination of information, to promote learning, culture and development."[2]

Unfortunately, the problem is even more complex than it might appear. What happens if someone hears some music, or reads an article, and then creates something new that is strongly influenced by that music or that article? Has he or she borrowed too much? What is too much? How can we tell? Who is to decide? There is no problem in deciding to take some action if there is extensive copying, word for word or note for note. But what if only the plot is used? What if only the distinctive counterpoint of the music is copied? What if a work is translated into another language? Surely there is some creative thought in choosing the best translation.

Suppose I have an idea for a new and useful invention of some kind? How do I protect that invention? If I write something, perhaps a book or some computer software that expresses or "carries out" that idea, what protection does the Copyright Act give me? Does it protect the idea or only the book that results from the idea?

Copyright law protects only the original contribution in a book or computer program that results from an idea, not the invention itself. There is another body of law to protect inventions — the law of patents — so it is, in fact, possible to protect the idea in a program with a patent and the actual code that expresses the idea by copyright.

Of course, there are no clear-cut answers to many of these questions. As with so many difficult conflicts, the courts ultimately have to decide, guided by the laws and regulations established by our elected representatives, and in some cases, by cultural tradition and precedent. In this book, we shall concentrate on the copyright and patent issues raised by computer software. Although the recent Copyright Act of 1976 did not specifically mention software, Congress intended that software should be brought under its umbrella of protection. Further refinements to the Copyright Act were made in 1980, but even then an important series of precedent-setting cases was needed to settle some of the unresolved issues. Important questions in the software area are still being litigated.

Although it is not necessary to become a computer expert to understand what the issues are, a certain amount of expertise is useful to understand what the courts are doing. Appendix A examines some of the underlying technology of computers in order to understand the issues involved in copyright and patent protection. The reader who is already knowledgeable about computers may wish to skim Appendix A, but those not comfortable with the technology should read the appendix.

The main part of the book deals with intellectual property issues, as they relate to software. Chapters 1 and 2 introduce the basic issues in copyright cases, and Chapter 3 is concerned with software-related patents. The rest of the book involves a more detailed discussion of copyright issues and litigation that have influenced the application of copyright law to software. Chapter 10, on the Clean Room Approach, describes one method that is being used to avoid copyright infringement allegations.

NOTES

1. This fictional illustration is based on the opening scenes of the movie "The Red Shoes."

2. The Whelan case. (This case is discussed in detail in Chapter 2.)

REFERENCE

Patterson, L. R. and Lindberg, S. W., *The Nature of Copyright: A Law of Users' Rights* (Athens: University of Georgia Press, 1991).

1

Legal Issues

Much of the litigation in the computer field is really not specific to computers. Many cases of breach of contract, misappropriation of trade secrets, and anti-trust violations fall under long-established legal precedents and principles. These cases happen to involve computers or computer companies, but the issues are standard fare for the legal profession. An important step in any litigation must be to recognize when the issues are specific to computers or some related technology, or when the computer is merely the product involved in an otherwise straightforward case of breach of contract. Many lawyers have indeed had to learn a great deal about the computer field in order to make these kinds of decisions.

For example, Company A agrees to market some software for Company B. Company A looks at an initial version of the software, decides that it looks pretty good, and signs a contract to put forth its best efforts to market Company B's software. After receiving the details about the software, Company A discovers that certain critical components of the software are not yet written, and other components are full of bugs. Company A refuses to market the software, claiming that the software provided is simply not marketable; it does not perform as warranted by Company B. Company B sues Company A for breach of contract. There are, of course, some technical issues to be clarified, such as the facts about components that were not delivered by Company B, the presence of bugs, and so on. Testimony from experts may be needed to advise the court about industry standards on the expected frequency of the existence of bugs and the nature of the software marketing environment, but once these computer-field-specific issues are determined, the court will decide the case using the principles and precedents of contract law.

What seems to make computer cases unique is that computers deal with information in a variety of forms, some of which look very much like literary expression, and others that look like parts of a machine. Machines can be patented, but what about the information in them, the software that makes them run? It has been argued that because a computer does nothing until the software is included, the software is an integral part of the machine; hence, it should be protected under patent law, not copyright law. Most of these distinctions and arguments come up as defensive techniques when copyright infringement has been charged. These issues require appropriate distinctions that have had to be sorted out one by one in precedent-setting cases. Other issues or arguments to be covered in the chapters that follow are:

Software is utilitarian; that is, its only purpose is to cause a machine to follow some instructions to solve a problem. There is no expression involved that deserves copyright protection.

If software is written in a high-level language on paper, punched on cards, or stored in random-access memory (RAM), it is different from machine-language zeros and ones stored in read-only memory (ROM), and different kinds of protection are needed.

While it is true that application programs written by users look like literary expression and should be copyrightable, operating systems are not visible to the user, and are really part of the computer, hence not subject to copyright protection.

If a company is licensed to copy another company's hardware, it is entitled to copy the microcode, also, because there is really only one way to write microcode efficiently. Microcode is also an integral part of the control unit, which is the heart of the computer; therefore, it is hardware.

What appears on the screen cannot be protected because it represents the idea or the design of the user interface, and not the expression. Besides, certain screen presentations are by now so standard that they can be used freely by anyone. In order to compete, another company must make its product look the same to the user. It is better for consumers if they do not have to learn several different ways of doing things.

How can a company undertake any kind of software development when it must always face the prospect that someone will claim copyright or patent infringement? Is there any way to somehow protect the process of software generation so copyright and patent infringement charges are simply recognized as untenable? Can this be done without incurring unreasonable expense?

Most of these issues have been considered by the courts and settled, at least until someone comes up with new facts or novel ways to argue against the court decisions. Some issues have not yet been tested in the courts or not yet settled definitively. We can expect to hear much more about them in the near future. I should make it clear that in general, I do not agree with many of the implied conclusions of the questions raised above. These questions are drawn from some of the cases discussed in the chapters that follow. They are raised here to suggest the kinds of questions the courts have been asked to resolve. If you have been comfortable so far with the references to software and other computer issues, by all means read on. If not, be sure to read Appendix A to get some useful background material in this area.

The software industry is now a major force in our economy, and issues of intellectual property protection will certainly shape the computer industry's future. If appropriate copyright or patent protection were not available, the software industry could very well cease to exist. At the very least, it would have to undergo severe changes. The problem is that it only takes a couple of minutes to make a copy of a software product. Then a disguised version that can be made to appear quite different from the original can be generated in a matter of days, or even hours, with the aid of a good utility program written for that purpose. Such a disguised version could easily be marketed as a new product, without the investment of effort and creativity that went into the original product.

This means that the lead time that the author was counting on before competitive products would appear on the market is simply not there. Who is going to invest the effort to create new and innovative products if competing products can appear almost immediately with essentially no effort?

2

Idea or Expression?

One of the most fundamental issues in copyright law is the distinction between an idea and the expression of that idea. An idea that leads to a particular kind of invention can be patented, while the expression of an idea must be copyrighted to be protected.

To illustrate the difference between patent protection and copyright protection, suppose that someone came up with a new method for coating a padlock with a rubber substance so that it will not damage the paint on any surface against which it might bump. Assuming that this was, in fact, a novel idea, a suitable application outlining the coating process could be submitted to the Patent Office, checked against the "prior art," and used as the basis for issuing a patent. At that point, no one could use that method without a license from the patent holder.

In contrast, suppose that someone created a television commercial around the idea of a committee meeting in which a member extols the virtues of a particular product. The idea of such a committee meeting probably does not satisfy the conditions for any patent consideration, but the script for the commercial could be copyrighted as a particular expression of the idea. Someone else could use the same idea and write a different script for it without challenge, as long as the new script was in fact independently created.

For another example, suppose a person comes up with a novel way to use a thumbprint for identification, as part of a security system for banks. In order to implement the new method, the inventor decides to use a computer chip in the recognition device. Of course there is a program in the computer chip to control its actions of scanning the thumbprint, analyzing it, and comparing it to stored images of thumbprints of authorized people. A patent application could describe the invention introduced in the device, such as the particular method of analysis used in reducing the thumbprint to a pattern so it could be compared against the stored patterns of authorized thumbprints. The patent application might go so far as to include some new method to be used to compare thumbprint images, which probably would not match exactly, but could be "scored" in some way as being "close enough" or "not close enough" to authorize entrance to areas in the bank. On the other hand, the specific computer program written to be used inside the device would probably not be part of the patent because there would be many ways to write the program, and because the program would in itself not introduce anything novel. The program would probably be copyrighted as the expression of the method described in the patent claims. Someone else with permission to use the method covered by the patent could write his or her own program without violating the protection afforded by the copyright.

Patent protection requires that an invention be novel, useful, and not obvious to "one skilled in the art." In return, once a patent is issued, no one else is allowed to use the same invention without permission for 17 years. A patent provides very strong protection because any unauthorized use, manufacture, or sale of the patented invention is illegal, even if the invention was independently created. On the other hand, copyright protection covers only a particular expression of an idea, does not protect against independent creation, and is subject to certain "fair use" limitations. Copyright protection does last for 50 years after the death of the author, however.[1] We shall consider software patent protection, a rapidly growing field, in the next chapter.

Although the distinction between an idea and its expression was clarified in a legal case as far back as 1879, Congress restated this distinction in the Copyright Act of 1976 with the explicit caution (17 U.S.C. § 102(b) [1982]): "In no case does copyright protection for an original work of authorship extend to any idea, procedure, process, system, method of operation, concept, principle, or discovery, regardless of the form in which it is described, explained, illustrated, or embodied in such work."

In each case of alleged copyright infringement there must be a determination of the idea or method, and the copyrighted expression. The 1879 case always referred to in such decisions is *Baker* v. *Selden*, in which Selden had copyrighted a book that described a simplified accounting method he had developed, and that included as part of his description some exemplary "blank forms," that is, pages with ruled lines and recommended headings. Baker then produced an accounting book that used essentially the same accounting method as Selden's and included pages that reproduced Selden's blank forms.

Baker v. Selden

Case: *Baker* v. *Selden*,
101 U. S. 99 (1879)

Date: January 19, 1880

Summary: Selden published a book describing a particular method of bookkeeping, including some blank forms (including headings for the columns, etc.) that were to be used to implement the method. Baker published his own book based on a similar method, but included a very similar form. Selden claimed copyright infringement, especially in the use of the similar form.

Decision: The Supreme Court reversed the decision of the Appeals Court, and found that the blank forms were not copyrightable. The copyright in the book to which they were attached did not extend to the forms; to do so would be using copyright protection to limit the public's right to practice the art described in the book.

Apparently everyone agreed that the method Selden had described was not copyrightable (because methods are not copyrightable), even though Selden's written text describing the method was copyrightable. Baker had not copied that descriptive text, but Selden argued that the blank forms were also part of his text, and, hence, Baker had no right to reproduce them in his book. The court decided in favor of Baker, that is, that the blank forms were necessary to the method: "Where the art it teaches cannot be used without employing the methods and diagrams used to illustrate the book, or such as are similar to them, such methods and diagrams are to be considered as necessary incidents to the art, and given to the public."

A similar issue came up in a very important and controversial software copyright case, *Whelan Associates, Inc.* v. *Jaslow Dental Laboratory, Inc. et al.*, which shall be referred to here as "Whelan ."

Whelan

Case: *Whelan Assoc.* v. *Jaslow Dental Laboratory, Inc.,*
797 F.2d 1222 (3rd Cir. 1986), cert denied, 479 U.S. 1031 (1987)

Date: August 4, 1986

Original decision: 609 F. Supp. 1325 (E. D. Pa. 1985)

Summary: Elaine Whelan, employed by Strohl Systems, developed a program for Jaslow Dental Laboratory for the operation of a dental laboratory, which ran on an IBM Series 1 computer. She later formed Whelan Associates, and both Jaslow and Whelan marketed the program, Dentalab. Jaslow realized that there would be a larger market for such a program on a more commonly used computer, and arranged for the creation of a corresponding dental office management program, Dentcom, in a different language, for the other computer. When they had a falling out, Jaslow sued Whelan for trade secret violation, and Whelan counter-sued for violation of the copyright on Dentalab. The district court found that Jaslow had violated the copyright, and Jaslow appealed. The primary issue was whether copyright protection covers only the literal elements of a literary work, or also the "overall structure and organization."

Decision: The Appeals Court affirmed the judgement of the District Court in favor of Whelan Associates.

In that case, as in the SAS Institute case, the issue revolved around copyright infringement assertions even when it was very clear that no code was copied and used directly.

SAS Institute

Case: *SAS Institute, Inc.* v. *S & H Computer Systems, Inc.,*
605 F. Supp. 816 (M. D. Tenn., 1985)

Date: March 6, 1985

Summary: SAS Institute had developed a statistical analysis package for IBM computers. S&H Computer Systems obtained a license for that package, and with it some of the source code. They later marketed a product called INDAS for Digital Equipment Corp. (DEC) equipment, which was found to be substantially similar to the SAS Institute package. The issues here included the question of whether the development of a new program based on an actual copy of the source code of an earlier one, but targeted for a different computer and written in a different language, would constitute the creation of a "derivative work." The court had to decide, therefore, whether nonliteral elements of the original program, such as the overall design and the choices of file structure and subroutine organization, were copied. Also involved was the amount of similarity needed to qualify for "substantial similarity."

Decision: The court found that S&H Computer Systems had indeed infringed the copyright of SAS Institute, and an injunction was issued against the marketing of INDAS, or any other product derived from INDAS or the SAS product.

In both cases, while it was clear that the alleged infringer had access to the original code, the version claimed to have been written in violation of the copyright protection was developed for a different computer, using a different language. Clearly, the actual new source code would be different from the original source code. The court had to decide, therefore, whether nonliteral elements of the original program, such as the overall design and the choices of file structure and subroutine organization, were copied. The nonliteral elements represented a level of abstraction away from the literal code; they were, in the words of the Whelan court, the "structure (or sequence and organization)" of the program, terms that the court used interchangeably. This abstraction is the basis for most of the controversy about the Whelan decision.

We shall return to the question of overall structure and organization in Chapter 7. What is meant by that phrase is the general organization of a large program into subroutines, the flow of execution among these subroutines, choices of data files and their organization, and so on.

With regard to the issue of the idea versus the expression, the Court of Appeals in the Whelan case clarified the distinction as follows:

Just as *Baker* v. *Selden* focused on the end sought to be achieved by Selden's book, the line between idea and expression may be drawn with reference to the end sought to be achieved by the work in question. In other words, the purpose or function of a utilitarian work would be the work's idea, and everything that is not necessary to that purpose or function would be part of the expression of the idea. . . . Where there are various means of achieving the desired purpose, then the particular means chosen is not necessary to the purpose: hence, there is expression, not idea.

The court goes on, in a footnote to that opinion: "This test is necessarily difficult to state, and it may be difficult to understand in the abstract. . . . The idea of the Dentalab program was the efficient management of a dental laboratory. . . . Because that idea could be accomplished in a number of different ways with a number of different structures, the structure of the Dentalab program is part of the program's expression, not its idea."

An important lesson here is that the existence of a number of ways to express an idea shows that none of those ways is required for the idea. Because none of those ways can be claimed to be part of the idea, these expressions can be copyrighted.

As we shall see, however, much depends on the level of abstraction, or conversely the level of detail, that is used in specifying the idea. In Whelan, the idea was identified as "efficient management of a dental laboratory." If it had been stated as "the efficient management of a dental laboratory with three chairs, and including provision for timely notice to patients in advance of appointments," the set of choices available to the system designer in expressing the idea would have been somewhat restricted. More detail in identifying the idea would have reduced the choices still further. It is not easy to determine where to draw that line.

One aspect that needs clarification, and that has led some to disagree with the Whelan opinion, is whether the Whelan court required that there be only one idea for a program (in this case, the efficient management of a dental laboratory). If so, then everything else is expression. Would the court have accepted several "levels of abstraction," so that there could be ideas at various levels, with multiple choices for each, leading to multiple expressions, each of which might, in fact, contain ideas at the next level? Of course, some critics question whether any abstraction above the level of the program source code should be protectable. We shall return to these questions in Chapter 8.

Another pair of cases shows how fine a line can be drawn in the area of idea versus expression. A 1989 case in Federal District Court,

Manufacturers Technologies, Inc. v. *CAMS, Inc.*, was concerned with software designed to enable users to estimate the cost of machining manufactured parts, as opposed to manual calculation.

MTI/CAMS

Case: *Manufacturers Technologies, Inc.* v. *CAMS, Inc.*,
          706 F. Supp. 984 (D. Conn. 1989)

Date: January 30, 1989

Summary: COSTIMATOR was a program developed for Manufacturers Technologies, Inc. (MTI) in 1982 and 1983. Its purpose was to assist in estimating the cost of machining a manufactured part. The defendants, who were previously sales representatives of MTI, developed and marketed similar programs, QC and RAPIDCOST, and were sued by MTI for copyright infringement. The issues included: (1) whether a single copyright registration for a program extends beyond the source and object code to the screen displays it generates, (2) whether the sequencing and flow of the screen displays communicated to the user a view of how cost-estimates should be created and therefore deserved copyright protection, or were dictated solely by functional considerations, and (3) whether certain aspects of the screen display, such as a two-column alphabetical listing of machine-shop departments, were entitled to copyright protection.

Decision: The court decided in favor of the plaintiff, MTI. It stated that MTI's copyright had been infringed, and enjoined the defendant from any further activity in marketing their programs. With respect to the three issues above, the court decided for (1) that a single copyright registration of a computer program would accomplish the registrations of both the program itself and the screen presentation. For (2) the court determined that the sequencing and flow of the screen displays did communicate to the user a view of how cost-estimates should be created and, therefore, deserved copyright protection. On (3) the results were mixed — some aspects of the screen display were entitled to copyright protection and some were not. The two-column alphabetical listing as such had no original authorship and did not deserve protection.

One of the main issues was whether a sequence of computer screen displays was copyrightable, and if so, when copying them constituted infringement of the copyright. The screen displays were registered as "compilations," which under the copyright code are defined as: "a work formed by the collection and assembling of pre-existing materials or of data that are selected, coordinated, or arranged in such a way that the resulting work as a whole constitutes an original work of authorship."

Compilations are given limited protection under copyright law because the originality (if any) is in the bringing together and the organization of pre-existing materials. In this case, however, the court found that:

The defendant has failed to rebut the presumption of copyright validity of this aspect [the flow and sequencing] of the screen displays. The flow of the plaintiff's screen displays reflect plaintiff's creative manner of expressing how the process of cost-estimating should be accomplished. By design, the COSTIMATOR program and its screen displays used in the creating of an estimate sequence drive the user's thought processes through a number of manufacturing and engineering decisions, thereby expediting the process of creating a cost-estimate and communicating to the user the manner in which a cost-estimate should be derived.

In 1978, in *Synercom Technology, Inc.* v. *University Computing Co.*, a company named EDI was charged with copying various parts of Synercom's manuals and Synercom input formats.

Synercom

Case: *Synercom Technology, Inc.* v. *University Computing Co.*,
           462 F. Supp. 1003 (N. D. Texas, 1978)

Date: August 24, 1978

Summary: University Computing, in an agreement with EDI, an
           engineering company, marketed a program that accepted
           input formatted according to published requirements of a
           program previously marketed by Synercom. Also at issue
           were the copyrighted manuals. The primary issue was

whether the sequence and ordering of the data was protectable by Synercom, that is, were they ideas or expression.

Decision: The court decided that the sequence and ordering of the data was the idea, hence not copyrightable, and even if that were not correct, formats are not copyrightable. According to the court's reasoning, "in the usual case sequence, choice, and arrangement have only stylistic significance, rather than constituting . . . the essence of the expression." Thus, EDI had violated the copyright on the manuals, but not on the data formats.

EDI's program included a preprocessor, a program that would digest the input data and prepare it for subsequent processing. This program expected the input data to be sequenced exactly as Synercom's program instructions and input formats directed it to be sequenced. Although the court found that there could have been over 3 million different sequences, and EDI used precisely the one that Synercom had used, the presiding judge ruled that only the sequence had been copied, and the sequence was the idea, not the expression of the idea, and, therefore, there was no infringement for that reason.[2] Thus, a fine line is drawn.

It is not surprising that other judges have found that the Synercom ruling was not necessarily a precedent that would serve as a useful guideline. According to the Appellate Court opinion in the Whelan case,

Central to [the Synercom judge's] analysis was his conviction that the organization and structure of the input formats was inseparable from the idea underlying the formats. Although the court acknowledged that in some cases structure and sequence might be part of expression, . . . it stated that in the case of input formats, structure and organization were inherently part of the idea. The court put its position in the form of a powerful rhetorical question: "if sequencing and ordering [are] expression, what separable idea is being expressed?" . . . To the extent that *Synercom* rested on the premise that there was a difference between the copyrightability of sequence and form in the computer context and in any other context, we think that it is incorrect. . . . the Copyright Act of 1976 demonstrates that Congress intended sequencing and ordering to be protectible [sic] in the appropriate circumstances, . . . and the computer field is not an exception to this general rule.

The Whelan court agreed, therefore, with the decision in MTI/CAMS, that sequence and organization is part of the creative expression of some more abstract idea, and hence copyrightable.

One aspect of the Synercom ruling is particularly difficult to accept. In concluding that sequence is the only aspect that was copied from the input formats, the court implicitly assumed that the input variables used by the Synercom programmers were clearly the only possible variables that could have been used as input, and that precisely the number called for by Synercom was required. In fact, it is much more likely that many other combinations of other variables could have served as input data, with the remaining variables computed from the ones chosen. In other words, it could be argued that the existence of a sequence, together with its format, was the idea, but the choice of which sequence and which variables to include in it was the expression.

One might conclude that the judge in the Synercom case took a simplistic view of program design. Of course, the outcome of that particular case probably would not have been different, given the conclusion that there was infringement of the copyright on the manual, but the precedent it set with regard to input formats continues to affect other cases. This is perhaps unavoidable in a field where the issues are still being clarified, and there may not yet be enough definitive cases.

As a general standard for distinguishing between an idea and various forms of its expression, the following passage appears in the opinion by Judge Learned Hand in *Nichols* v. *Universal Pictures Corporation*. It is referred to as his "abstractions test": "Upon any work, and especially upon a play, a great number of patterns of increasing generality will fit equally well, as more and more of the incident is left out. The last may perhaps be no more than the most general statement of what the play is about, and at times might consist of only its title; but there is a point in this series of abstractions where they are no longer protected, since otherwise the playwright could prevent the use of his ideas, to which, apart from their expression, his property is never extended."

Nichols

Case: *Nichols* v. *Universal Pictures Corp.*,
           45 F.2d 119 (2d Cir.), Cert denied, 282 U.S. 902 (1930)

Date: November 10, 1930

Summary: Anne Nichols, the author of a popular play, "Abie's Irish Rose," claimed that a movie produced by Universal, "The Cohens and The Kellys," infringed on her copyright. Though the plots and some of the characters had some similarities, there were also differences. The issues included the level of abstraction at which the differences and similarities occurred, and what aspects of the play the public had a right to use.

Decision: The court found that there was no infringement.

This helps to explain why it is sometimes difficult to decide what the appropriate idea is. There is almost a continuum between the title of a work and the full detail, with the title containing no detail, but each step away from the title involving more and more details of the structure, relationships between the components, and so on. The line between the idea and the expression lies somewhere between the two extremes. It is not surprising that opposing litigants will assert different versions of the idea when they argue their positions.

It is not uncommon for a programmer or other technical witness to be asked what appears to be a simple question, such as: "What is the basic idea in a user interface?" Other questions might be: "What is the idea behind using an icon?" or "Is the use of a wastebasket on the desktop a good idea?" It may well be that the questioner is not at all interested in how good the idea is, but is really aiming at getting the technical person to label some pertinent aspect of that particular litigation as an idea, as opposed to part of the expression of the idea. Later, during the actual trial arguments, the witness would be quoted as supporting the view of that party to the litigation as to what the idea is, to help draw the line between the idea and the expression that we have been discussing. Probably the best stance for the witness (who is most likely not a lawyer) to take is to point out from the beginning that the words being discussed are not being used in any legal sense. Computer scientists and programmers do not make the distinction between "idea" and "expression" when developing a program or system; it is really a legal distinction. Recent copyright cases involving computer programs have actually been tending to permit more and more expert testimony in areas previously reserved for jurors, but potential expert witnesses should be aware of the dangers here.

Rather than label any particular aspect as either idea or expression, what the designer is making is a hierarchy of choices. Such a hierarchy is often referred to as a "tree," with each node of the tree being expanded into a number of further choices at the next level. Whether the lawyers want to label any node on the tree an idea is up to them and their specific goals, but it will not be based on technical grounds.

It would often appear to be easy to state the purpose, and, hence, the idea, of a particular body of computer software, but that is not always so. Consider the case of *NEC, Inc.* v. *Intel, Inc.*, decided in 1988 in the Federal District Court in San Jose, California. Part of the case revolved around the idea of the microcode used in the control unit of a particular computer.

Intel

Case: *NEC, Inc.* v. *Intel, Inc.*,
           1989 W.L. 67434 (N. D. Cal. Feb. 7, 1989)

Date: February 6, 1989

Summary: Intel had granted NEC a license to use its architecture and microcode for the 8088 and 8086 chips, and for improvements to them. NEC used its knowledge of that microcode for its more advanced processors based on that architecture, and Intel claimed that its copyright on the microcode was infringed. The issues included: (1) whether microcode was copyrightable, and (2) whether Intel had properly protected its copyright by insisting on the copyright marker being placed on the chips.

Decision: Intel's copyright was ruled invalid and not infringed, but Intel did succeed in establishing that microcode is copyrightable.

Intel argued that the purpose, or idea, of the microcode was to allow the control unit to interpret the intent of the machine instruction codes, such as Add and Subtract. NEC defined the purpose of the microcode in question as allowing the control unit in a particular design of the computer to interpret the intent of the instruction codes.

The difference here was that Intel did not include the constraint of using a particular hardware design, and argued that among the many ways to express the idea one could start with a different architecture. If that were done, very different software would be created in the expression of the idea, that is, in the microcode, to go with that different hardware.

NEC argued, on the other hand, that because it was previously licensed to copy the Intel hardware (in this case, the Intel 8088 and 8086 microprocessors), it could choose to use that hardware, greatly reducing the number of possible ways to express the microcode. NEC then argued that there was essentially only one way (or very few ways) to write much of the microcode, given the constraints of the hardware they were using. We shall return to the issue of "only one way to write the microcode" in this case when we take up the merger issue later in this chapter. The point here is that two participants in a dispute may put forth quite different definitions of the idea involved in the case. From these definitions of the idea may flow very different interpretations as to how many choices were available, and hence what expressions may be protected by copyright.

As another example, we find in the Broderbund opinion that "the idea of "Print Shop" [a computer program] is the creation of greeting cards, banners, posters and signs that contain infinitely variable combinations of text, graphics, and borders. A rival software publisher is completely free to market a program with the same underlying idea, but it must express the idea through a substantially different structure."

Broderbund

Case: *Broderbund Software, Inc. v. Unison World, Inc.,*
           648 F. Supp. 1127 (N. D. Cal. 1986)

Date: October 8, 1986

Summary: Broderbund had developed a program for Apple computers to produce greeting cards and signs, and had discussed with Unison World a contract under which the latter would produce an IBM PC version of the program. When negotiations broke down, the Unison programmers continued to use information obtained from Broderbund. When Unison released their product, Broderbund sued for copyright infringement. The issues included merger of idea and expression and support of the Whelan decision regarding the idea of a program and its relationship to its purpose.

Decision: Unison World had infringed the copyright on the audiovisual displays of the Broderbund program.

We note that the court might have decided in the Broderbund case that the idea of a program like "Print Shop" would be the creation of greeting cards, banners, posters, and signs, but without the added property of allowing "infinitely variable combinations of text, graphics, and borders." The difference then is that there would be a far greater number of possible computer programs whose function was only to produce greeting cards and similar items than there would be with the additional requirement that there be "infinitely variable combinations of text, graphics, and borders." In this specific case, there were apparently enough possible programs satisfying the additional requirement to carry the day. This case does illustrate, however, that it is not always obvious what the appropriate idea should be from which expressions were generated.

THE MERGER ARGUMENT

An important test in the distinction between idea and expression is the number of ways in which a work can be expressed. If there are many ways, many choices, then we are dealing with expression. What if there are not many choices?

Suppose, for example, that a manufacturer of a very special kind of video-game cartridge to be used with a game computer has designed the cartridge, the game computer hardware, and the software so there is only one sequence of data that the computer in the cartridge can transmit to the game computer that will correctly start the action of the cartridge. A competitor wishing to compete by selling compatible cartridges would have to know the correct sequence of data to transmit, or the competing cartridges could not activate the game computer properly. Thus the competitor might argue that it is necessary that the program sequence used in the cartridge to generate the specific sequence of data not be protectable. If it were, and if access were withheld from the public, there could be no competition in the market for video-game cartridges.

The argument the competitor would make would be that to protect the program sequence under the Copyright Act would in effect protect the idea of starting the cartridge action. Anyone learning what the correct program sequence should be and then trying to write a program to be used in the cartridge would necessarily produce code that would be almost identical with the protected program. If this were considered a violation of the Copyright Act, it would amount to using that act, with its very long period of protection, to preclude someone else's use of the idea, and thus give the more inclusive kind of protection that comes with patents. The restriction would have been invoked without having to satisfy the more stringent tests of novelty, usefulness, and non-obviousness that patent protection requires. This line of reasoning, that the idea and the expression have thus "merged," is called "the merger argument."

One answer is that the competing company is free to develop its own computer system, that is, its own game computer hardware and software and its own cartridge and triggering program sequence. Then it would have as much freedom as the original company to decide on the required program sequence. The original designer had a great many choices to begin with because the game computer hardware and software and the cartridge design were all being designed at the same time. That the competing company wants to make the decision to compete in the video-cartridge market using the same hardware and software is a business decision, and does not justify copying. The company is free to try to license the code from the original company as well. If that company refuses, there is then a possible question of monopoly power, and antitrust law might be invoked, but that is a separate question. The person supplying this answer does not buy the merger argument in such a case.

Another answer, however, says that once the hardware is on the market, the competitor should be free to compete in the market for video cartridges that are compatible with that game computer hardware. If there were a large number of program sequences that could correctly activate the game computer, then the competitor need not and should not copy the particular expression used by the original company. However, if there are only a very few ways (or just one) that can work, then indeed the idea and the expression have merged, and a competitor should not be stopped under the Copyright Act from using one of those few ways.

The merger argument is often used in copyright defense arguments. One answer to it is to demonstrate that there are, in fact, a large number of ways to write the relevant computer programs, all of which may be expressions of the same idea but different from each other. Here we run into the question of what it means to be different, or conversely, what it means to be similar. The relevant concepts in this area will be discussed in Chapter 7.

Before even demonstrating that the relevant idea can be expressed in a number of ways, however, there must be some agreement as to what the idea is. As we indicated earlier, in the *NEC* v. *Intel* case, NEC argued that the idea included a specific choice of hardware architecture that it was licensed to use, while Intel argued that NEC was obliged to avoid or modify that hardware, if necessary, to avoid copyright infringement in writing the microcode. The court agreed with NEC that the idea could include the constraint that a particular hardware architecture was to be used because they were licensed by Intel to use it. This reduced considerably (almost entirely in some cases, the court concluded) the possible variations in the microcode sequences that one could write. In the Memorandum of Decision that accompanied the judgment, the court wrote: "Having granted to NEC a license to duplicate the hardware of its 8086/88 to the extent comprehended by the Intel patents, and having conceded at trial that NEC had a right to duplicate the hardware of the 8086/88 because it was not otherwise protected by Intel, Intel is in no position to challenge NEC's right to use the aspects of Intel's microcode that are mandated by such hardware" (p. 34).

The apparent assumption in this opinion is that someone may voluntarily choose to impose whatever constraints are legal on his or her work before beginning to develop a potentially infringing work. As we have seen, if enough constraints are imposed, one can then argue that there are so few choices left that the result is bound to look extremely similar.

An alternate assumption could be made that once one knows of the existence of copyright protection on a work, which was the case in *NEC v. Intel*, one should make those choices that are available so as to avoid infringing. In this case, that would have meant designing a different architecture for the chip, which Intel itself eventually did for later versions of its own processors. NEC made several useful modifications to the chip architecture, but almost nothing that would have made the microcode take a radically different form.

In discussing another constraint voluntarily imposed by NEC, that is, its restricted use of a greatly expanded area for the storage of microcode which was available to it, the court found that "This also was a legitimate constraint; NEC was not obliged to avoid the similarity that other constraints imposed by creating a larger microcode."

Efficiency is another self-imposed constraint that is sometimes invoked. There are, of course, possible objectives other than efficiency, such as reliability, time to market, and ease of installation and maintenance. There are also different kinds of efficiency, including the use of available storage (both primary and secondary storage), computation time, and avoidance of errors by users.

Even granted that everyone wants to make the program under development as efficient as possible, one wonders if that is enough justification to argue that there are very few ways to express an idea efficiently, and then invoke the merger argument. This apparently works with some courts, as we see in the recent opinion of the Appeals Court in the *Computer Associates* v. *Altai* case:

Another justification for linking structural economy with the application of the merger doctrine stems from a program's essentially utilitarian nature and the competitive forces that exist in the software marketplace. . . . Efficiency is an industry-wide goal. Since there may be only a limited number of efficient implementations for any given task, it is quite possible that multiple programmers, working independently, will design the identical method employed in the allegedly infringed work. Of course, if this is the case, there is no copyright infringement. . . . Under these circumstances, the fact that two programs contain the same efficient structure may as likely lead to an inference of independent creation as it does to one of copying.

Altai

Case: *Computer Associates Int'l, Inc.* v. *Altai, Inc.*, 22 F.3d 32 (2d Cir. 1992), 832 F. Supp. 50 (E.D.N.Y. 1991)

Date: June 22, 1992

Original decision: August 9, 1991

Summary: A former employee of Computer Associates (CA) took with him some source code for an operating-system interface program when he went to work for Altai. He copied part of this code to develop an operating-system interface program for Altai, although no one at Altai knew that he had done this. When it was discovered, a clean-room version was developed by Altai to replace the program he had written. The issue was whether this new program was sufficiently different and untainted to avoid further claims of copyright infringement.

Decision: The District Court agreed with CA that Altai's first version of the program had infringed their copyright, but determined that the new program did not infringe. The Appeals Court affirmed that decision.

This is, indeed, a slippery slope, leading to the inevitable claim: "It may appear from the choices I made in writing my program that I copied the other person's work, but really, I did not. It was the only way to make the program efficient." It is a business decision that a product have certain performance characteristics. That decision ought not to confer the right to arbitrarily appropriate someone else's expression. If the original author can show that there are more than just a few other ways to express the idea, then the desire to compete in the marketplace should not grant someone else the right to choose only the one expression that has been successful. We shall see in discussing several other cases that the business decision to provide the same user interface or the ability to run the same application programs as a successful product so as to attract customers has not been deemed sufficient reason to justify copying. The same reasoning should have been applied here.

NOTES

1.   In the case of a "work for hire," copyright protection extends for the lesser of 75 years from publication or 100 years from creation.

2.   There was in the Synercom case plenty of cause for determining infringement on other grounds, but that is not the issue here.

3

Software Patents

It will be useful to review the status of software patent protection at this point. It was mentioned earlier that the Copyright Act of 1976 did not explicitly cover software copyrights, but that this was accomplished in a revision of the act in 1980. As a result of the early recognition of the need, Congress established a special National Commission on New Technological Uses of Copyrighted Works (CONTU), and their 1978 report was the basis of the 1980 changes. In fact, because of the almost complete lack of legislative history regarding software copyrightability, the CONTU report is often cited in its place. In 1978, when the report was issued, CONTU considered it quite unlikely that patents would become much of an issue in software protection:

It is still unclear whether a patent may ever be obtained for a computer program. On three occasions the Supreme Court has considered cases involving program patents [footnote omitted]. In each it has found the programs before it to be ineligible for such protection. However, the Court has never addressed the broader question whether programs are patentable subject matter. The holdings of these three cases, although carefully limited in scope, make it appear that it would be difficult for any applicant to secure a patent in a program, since novel and useful mathematical formulas may not be patented. . . . Even if patents prove available in the United States, only the very few programs which survive the rigorous application and appeals procedure could be patented. Once such protection attached, of course, all others would be barred from using the patented process, even if independently developed.[1]

According to one report, legal advice about the difficulty involved in obtaining patents "kept Dan Bricklin, developer of VisiCalc, the first personal computer spreadsheet, from seeking patent protection for his program. . . . But since a landmark Supreme Court decision in 1981 that upheld a patent for a computer algorithm, the use of patents to protect software has increased."[2]

The fields of patent law and copyright law have both been evolving for a long time, but they were generally dealing with different kinds of objects. Copyright law is usually associated with literary expression, such as books and poetry, and patent law has dealt with processes, machines, composition of matter, and so on. Software, which can be viewed as implementing a process, brings the two legal disciplines much closer together, and the appropriate distinction is not clear in many cases. The dichotomy between idea and expression originated in copyright law, and it is useful as a rule of thumb to distinguish potentially patentable subject matter from copyrightable expression. On the other hand, not every idea is eligible for patent protection. There are quite stringent conditions to be satisfied before an idea becomes a patentable invention.

The 1981 Supreme Court opinion referred to above is *Diamond* v. *Diehr*, in which the court took the position that while a mathematical formula, or algorithm, in general is not patentable, the use of a formula in a patent claim does not necessarily invalidate that claim. If the claim uses the formula or algorithm in a process that would be patentable when considered as a whole, or is performing a function that would normally be considered patentable, then the use of the formula does not change that determination. This opened up patent protection to the entire field of software algorithms, subject, of course, to the standard criteria for patentability — that the process be novel, useful, and not obvious to someone skilled in the art.[3]

Diehr

Case: *Diamond, Commissioner of Patents and Trademarks* v. *Diehr,* 450 U.S. 175 (1981)

Date: March 3, 1981

Summary: A patent for a rubber-curing process was rejected by the U.S. Patent & Trademark Office, at least in part because part of the process was in the form of a mathematical formula, and hence not patentable.

Decision: Although the Supreme Court held that a mathematical formula per se was not patentable, a process that includes the use of such a formula and is otherwise patentable is not precluded from being patentable for that reason. In this case, the rubber-curing process was patentable, notwithstanding the use of a mathematical computation and a digital computer.

Patents provide powerful protection, and, therefore, are very desirable. The difficulty in preparing a patent application has always been the necessity of proving that the invention is novel and non-obvious. Between 1980 and 1990, however, over 5,500 patents were issued for software-related inventions, compared to about 4,500 patents, primarily hardware, issued by the same part of the U.S. Patent & Trademark Office (PTO) in the 18 years preceding 1980. In fact, the number of application filings is increasing at a rapid rate: 1,500 of the 5,500 software-related patents issued between 1980 and 1990 were granted in 1989 and 1990 alone. Since 1990, around 2,500 software-related patents have been granted each year.

In an article entitled "Software Industry in Uproar Over Recent Rush of Patents" in the *New York Times* (May 12, 1989), Lawrence M. Fisher compares recent patents issued for software, such as for the use of windows on a display screen, to a patent "for the opening notes of Beethoven's Fifth Symphony." The concern is that software may be patented by someone who will then suddenly start to demand royalties from those who are freely using techniques long considered to be in the public domain. Behind these concerns is a belief that the PTO does not have enough expertise in software to recognize old and well-known ideas that have been around for years and have been freely used by everyone. Even when an invention is really new and deserves patent protection, the procedure is secret and takes so long — years in most cases — that others are likely to come up with the same invention and find out only after several years of development and marketing that they have been infringing on someone else's patent.

It is not at all uncommon in science and technology for several people in different places to arrive at the same invention in a relatively short period of time. With ever-improving communication of ideas in the technical community, all these people are building on a similar base of experience. It is not surprising to find similar inventions springing up in several companies and/or universities within a few years of each other. As a result, the uncertainty of the patent situation is especially hard on small, newly formed companies. Customers are likely to avoid new software that may later turn out to be unavailable or unsupported because a small company infringed someone else's patent. Venture capital funding is often dependent on a new company's ability to obtain a patent for its own software as insurance.

Some companies are now applying for patents left and right, in order to have some of their own with which to bargain and/or trade in case they find themselves involved in an infringement lawsuit. Of course, this kind of activity is not new. In the hardware field, companies have often applied for many patents, primarily as incentives for others to cross-license patents back and forth with them. What is new is the frequency with which this has begun to happen in the software field. Particularly disturbing to software vendors is the length of time it takes to get a patent, often two to four years, compared to the rate of change in the field itself.

One thing competitors can do if they fear being accused of infringing is ask the PTO to re-examine a patent, and offer to help by pointing out prior art that might cause the PTO to disallow some or all of the claims in the patent application. Re-examination is seldom requested, however, because the initiator is excluded from the entire re-examination process. More often, the competitor will decide to wait until actual litigation is undertaken to present any prior art of which they are aware. In any case, two severe problems are the lack of any archive in which one might find information about prior art, and the impossibility of finding out about a patent application prior to its issuance so one could ask to have it evaluated more critically before costly litigation starts. Useful examples of prior art are most likely buried within application programs or system software, and known only to the authors in any detail. Because the software patent history is of such short duration (only about 14 years), the PTO certainly does not have a significant archive of its own. The burden is entirely on the person or organization wishing to demonstrate prior art to search out specific examples, without much help from any general archival process. It would be useful to the PTO and to the software industry if some database did exist. Creators of new techniques and inventions could then submit them for everyone else's use, perhaps after applying for their own patents. The primary need at this time is to make available information about the many ideas and techniques that are already in the public domain and that should not be patentable because of prior art. Of course, as patents are issued, they become part of the prior art, and they need to be accessible as well.

I have been instrumental recently in creating such a prior art database. With considerable industrial support and PTO encouragement, the Software Patent Institute (SPI) has been established in Ann Arbor, Michigan, with a specific goal of soliciting prior art, especially that generally regarded as "folklore," from software vendors, academics, publishers, and practitioners in the field. The resulting database is available for search requests from the PTO, to better judge what is novel, and to potential applicants for patents. As a result of a search of the database, some applicants may better anticipate being turned down on the basis of a lack of novelty, and they may decide not to apply at all.

Search requests may also be expected from litigants trying to establish that an allegedly infringed patent should not have been issued in the first place. It is too early to predict how effective challenging patents on the basis of prior art will be. Patent holders are legally entitled to a presumption of validity, and it is up to the challenger to prove invalidity. Because very few significant cases have arisen in the software field so far, it is hard to anticipate what will happen here, although the Compton case may point to some changes in the future.

In November 1993, Compton Encyclopedia, Inc., a subsidiary of The Tribune Company,[4] announced that it had obtained a patent[5] covering some basic techniques for searching and retrieving multi-media information from CD-ROM databases, and that it intended to enforce the patent by asking for royalties from licensees. An immediate uproar ensued, with many people coming up with evidence that they argued was prior art, which should invalidate the claimed invention. At issue was the future of a new field of application in the software field, a field that is currently one of the most active in the industry.

Bruce Lehman, commissioner of Patents and Trademarks, quickly ordered a reexamination of the Compton patent.[6] The re-examination notice cited a number of examples of prior art, and stated: "In view of the teachings of the prior art cited above, a substantial new question of patentability is raised as to claims 1 to 41 of U. S. Patent No. 5,241,671. Accordingly, Reexamination is ordered and all of the claims of [this patent] will be reexamined." In addition, an invitation was issued to the public to provide additional prior art, an unprecedented step for the PTO. Subsequent to this order, in March 1994, the PTO issued a news release stating: "All claims in Compton's multi-media patent issued in August

1993 have been rejected, on the grounds that they lack 'novelty' or are obvious in view of prior art."

Finally, on November 9, 1994, the PTO issued a news release stating:

The Patent and Trademark Office (PTO) announced today it has formally rejected all 46 claims in Compton's NewMedia software patent after an exhaustive reexamination that allowed greater than usual third-party participation in the process. . . . Compton's NewMedia was issued U.S. patent No. 5,241,671 on August 31, 1993, for a multimedia search and retrieval system. [PTO Commissioner] Lehman ordered the reexamination after the PTO discovered new information not considered by the patent examiner before issuing the multimedia patent.

On January 7, 1994, Lehman opened the reexamination proceedings to the public, welcoming any information the public wanted the agency to consider.

On March 23 the PTO rejected all 41 original claims. On June 23 Compton's filed a response, and on October 27 the agency rejected all claims. Compton's NewMedia and patent co-owner Encyclopedia Britannica have two months to appeal the decision to the PTO's Board of Appeals and Interference and after that to the courts.

One well-known patent case, *Honeywell, Inc.* v. *Sperry Rand Corp. et al.*, concluded in 1973, shows how a patent can be challenged even years after being issued. When John Mauchly and J. Presper Eckert invented and built the ENIAC computer at the University of Pennsylvania in the late 1940s, they obtained a patent on their invention that covered many aspects of the new computer. Years later, after the patent had been transferred to Remington Rand because it had acquired the company founded by Eckert and Mauchly, the successor company, the Sperry Rand Corporation, tried to collect royalties from several major computer manufacturers. Honeywell refused to pay royalties. Indeed, Honeywell took on the task of trying to prove that the patent was invalid. Honeywell attorneys found a reference in a book published in the early 1960s that mentioned a computer built by John V. Atanasoff at Iowa State University around 1940. They followed that lead, and discovered that before developing the ENIAC, Mauchly had visited Atanasoff at Iowa State University, and had seen and discussed Atanasoff's invention, a much smaller, but quite innovative computer, specifically designed to solve certain kinds of mathematical problems. In their patent application, Mauchly and Eckert claimed many of their own innovations on the ENIAC, but the judge ruled that they also had included some claims of invention that rightly belonged to Atanasoff, and that Mauchly had had an opportunity to observe Atanasoff's work during his visit to Iowa State University. Even though no patent had ever been obtained for the

Atanasoff computer, the court invalidated the ENIAC patent based in part on the Atanasoff work, because Honeywell had demonstrated that Eckert and Mauchly were not the sole inventors of the claimed invention. No royalties were paid.

ENIAC

Case: *Honeywell, Inc.* v. *Sperry Rand Corp. et al.*, 180 U.S.P.Q. 673, 1973 WL 903 (D.Minn.)

Date: October 19, 1973

Summary: Sperry Rand had acquired the patent previously obtained by J. Presper Eckert and John Mauchly, inventors of the ENIAC computer at the University of Pennsylvania. Illinois Scientific Developments, Inc., a subsidiary of Sperry Rand, charged Honeywell with infringement of the patent. Honeywell's defense was to argue that the patent was invalid. The latter's claim was based on knowledge that Mauchly was alleged to have obtained about a computer that had been built at Iowa State University by John V. Atanasoff. Atanasoff had built a computer to solve ordinary differential equations, and the computer had only partially worked. Eckert and Mauchly had included in their patent claims some inventions that Atanasoff argued were his.

Decision: The court found that because of the visit to Atanasoff, Mauchly had indeed claimed some of Atanasoff's ideas. The patent was declared not valid.

The prior art database that the Software Patent Institute is building might have made the job of discovering such prior art as the Atanasoff computer easier. While the SPI database cannot be expected to include all possible prior art, it should make it much easier for such references to be uncovered.

This illustrates that a patent can be challenged for lack of novelty — the patented invention simply is not new. The other criterion used to challenge a patent is that which requires an invention to be non-obvious to someone skilled in the art. This is not easy to establish, of course. Even if there were some agreement on who is skilled in the art, it is difficult to determine what invention is obvious to such a person. The test that the PTO uses to establish whether a claimed invention is obvious is to identify all relevant prior art and then ask whether the new invention is the result of a non-obvious step beyond the identified prior art. By this definition, the PTO examiners are the appropriate "persons of ordinary skill in the art" to make that determination. In many disciplines other than software, the background of PTO examiners closely matches the area of technology of the patent application. The PTO has few, if any, people with strong software backgrounds, however, and this understandably makes it quite difficult for the staff to make decisions in this area. Given the lack of known prior art in the software field and the lack of PTO expertise in the area, almost anything might seem to be a giant step forward. It is partly for these reasons that so many software patents based on inventions that seem obvious to software developers are being issued.

Another goal of the SPI is to arrange educational programs for the examiners of the PTO and others interested in the patent process, so they will be better able to recognize obvious software techniques and inventions. If this is successful, together with the SPI prior art database, the SPI hopes that the software-related patents that are issued in the future will only be those that are truly novel and non-obvious to those in the software community, as well as in the opinion of the PTO examiners.

It is encouraging that the PTO hired ten computer science graduates as trainee examiners in the summer of 1994. If successful, these trainees may become examiners after two years. In any case, their expertise is already available within the PTO.

An example of a recently granted software patent may illustrate a situation that has raised concerns in the software field. On February 21, 1989, Cary L. Queen was awarded Patent #4,807,182, which he had applied for on March 12, 1986. The patent was then assigned to Advanced Software, Inc. This patent describes a process for comparing two documents and identifies words and sentences that are different between them. (See Appendix B for a copy of the patent as issued.)

Software for comparing two files, or bodies of text, has existed for many years. In the UNIX™ environment, created in the early 1970s, a specific command, "diff," can be invoked with two file names; diff reports back each line in each file that differs from the corresponding line in the other file. One important use of such a command is to compare two versions of a document, perhaps edited by different people, to see what changes have been made. While there are many techniques for doing such a comparison, each has its own degree of efficiency. Writing some kind of program to accomplish this comparison is comparable to an exercise in a second course in programming, but the result of such a class exercise would most likely not compare well in efficiency and cost with the method described in this patent. This does illustrate, however, that the subject of the patent is probably not a great breakthrough in computer science.

What is introduced as novel in this patent application is the specific way the comparison function is applied to documents produced by word-processing software. In other words, the author recognized that word-processing software almost universally treats text as formed into words, sentences, and paragraphs, giving the text a special kind of structure. Word-processing software generally presents each paragraph to the user as a continuous stream of words and sentences on the display screen, so the insertion of a word, or even a single character, in the middle of a paragraph will cause the rest of the paragraph (and in some cases, even other text below that in the document), to be pushed down and reformatted, if necessary. The result might be that a word at the end of a visual line would now be wrapped around, that is, moved automatically to the next line, forcing one or more words from that line to be moved to the next, and so on. Earlier text processors, as distinguished from word processors, usually only modified the line or lines actually being changed, and wrap-around was up to the author to arrange by separate manipulations.

The author of this patent added to the usual comparison function the ability to consider an entire paragraph at a time, so that a word that was moved to the next line on the screen was still seen as being compared with the words in the previous line in the original document. The results were displayed in terms of the structure provided by the word processor; that is, the words and sentences that had changed between the two versions of the document were displayed, not just individual strings of characters out of context, as earlier programs had done.

This was the novel idea of the patent, and the PTO decided that it was indeed novel. One might question, however, whether it might have been obvious to someone outside the PTO who was skilled in the art. It is the kind of thing that would strike a computer programmer as obvious. In fact, most inventions are probably of that kind, but someone is the first to identify them as worth pursuing and developing. Patent protection rewards that person with the fruits of his or her persistence and ingenuity. On the other hand, using the PTO's test of asking whether the innovation is an obvious step beyond the known prior art, most people working in the field would indeed have concluded that this invention was obvious.

The particular patent being examined describes a specific method for accomplishing the comparison. It involves a programming technique known as hashing, and a particular way to use a central processing unit (CPU) interrupt mechanism to generate a second cursor on the screen,[7] because most display devices only provide for one cursor. In this context, hashing is used to locate lines and sentences that correspond in the relevant documents, so these lines and sentences can be compared in detail for differences. Blocks of similar, or different, text sequences are then identified in an efficient manner and reported out to the person running the program.

The patent, then, in its abstract, describes the following invention: "Method and apparatus for comparing original and modified versions of a document. The system of the present invention utilizes a hash number generator CPU to generate hash numbers for lines and sentences contained in the documents. Matching hash numbers are defined as anchorpoints and stored in an anchorpoint memory." The rest of the abstract gives more detail on the particular system being described (see Appendix B).

In an article in the April 17, 1989, issue of *Infoworld*, Rachel Parker says of the patent: "The broad patent protection granted to Advanced Software has startled [people] in the industry." Why are people so startled, and why is the software industry in an uproar over such developments? At least in part, there is a general lack of understanding over just how broad this protection is. How much does this particular patent protect for Advanced Software, Inc., for example, and how different does another comparison program have to be to not infringe on this patent? Is any comparison program for any computer in violation from now on? That would of course be worrisome, but in fact the situation does not appear to be that bad.

Patent #4,807,182 is structured like many other patents. After the usual abstract describing the invention very briefly come the drawings that are intended to illustrate the detailed description of the "preferred embodiment," which comes later. Drawings were originally intended under early patent law to show how to build the equipment or machine being described, but they are not very convincing when it comes to describing software. Most programmers would expect to see a flow diagram or other graphic representation of a program. Instead one finds what might almost pass for the components of a special-purpose computer that might have wired into it the function of the program being patented. One gets the impression that in order to fit the culture and history of the PTO, the software involved must be made to look as much like a machine as possible. The effect, of course, is to make the claimed invention more obscure.

After the drawings is a statement of the background of the invention. Here the inventor typically establishes the basis for the invention. This is where the limitations of the "prior art" are listed, preparing the way for the justification of the new invention. The patent will be justified in terms of the ways in which the limitations of earlier work are met, in a novel and non-obvious fashion. For the comparison program at hand, the argument is made that previous comparison programs have in fact existed, but they have been limited to "line by line comparison of the text . . . where each line is discrete and text does not wrap around the end of lines. . . . Another major flaw in prior art text comparison systems is that they generally produce as output only a listing of the lines that differ between the two files. Although the user may view both the original and the changed text, he cannot view that text in proper context in the document."

After the background section we find the Summary of the Invention, in which the preferred embodiment is described, although not yet in detail. The preferred embodiment is the "existence proof," as mathematicians would call it. This is the proof that the invention can in fact be implemented, because it gives one way to do it. Actually, the techniques presented in the summary, and the detailed description that follows, called the "description of the preferred embodiment" in patent parlance, are important in determining whether there is infringement — whether an alleged infringer has used the same subject matter that the patent owner claims as his invention. The actual claims of the patent will be discussed shortly. However, given the way that the owner of the patent in Appendix B has decided to claim his invention, the question of whether a product infringes will be judged by how close the product comes to performing each of the step-by-step functions presented in the claims, and whether that product used the exact same implementation described in the patent for carrying out each claimed function, or equivalent implementations. Of course, there is plenty of room for argument as to what is equivalent, but these are the guidelines.

It is interesting to read patent applications and watch for the ways in which the author describes something that can actually perform the claimed function, and yet tries to make the claimed invention as general as possible, so as to include all possible variants as equivalents. Thus, it is stated in column 11 of the current patent,

While the present invention has been particularly described with reference to FIGS. 1-5 and with emphasis on certain computer systems and peripheral devices, it should be understood that the figures are for illustration only and should not be taken as limitations upon the invention. In addition, it is clear that the methods and apparatus of the present invention have utility in any application where automatic test [sic] comparison is desired. It is contemplated that many changes and modifications may be made, by one of ordinary skill in the art, without departing from the spirit and scope of the invention as described above.

How wide a net is cast may only be settled by future negotiation and/or litigation.

Perhaps the most interesting part of any patent is the assertion of claims. In column 11 of the patent in Appendix B are the words, "I claim:" followed by 22 separate claims. This is where the inventor sets forth the specific allegedly novel and non-obvious aspects of the patent, which others must not practice without permission of some kind. The first 11 claims are directed to an "automated comparison system" and set forth the means comprising that system. The remaining claims are directed to a method for displaying the difference between two documents. They set forth the steps comprising the inventor's method.

Taken alone, the first claim (where the "first and second groups" referred to are the two documents being compared), is very comprehensive:[8]

1. An automated comparison system, comprising:
    input means for receiving commands, and for providing electronic signals representing a plurality of characters including words and sentences;
    memory means coupled to said input means for storing as binary representations at least first and second groups of said characters;
    processing means coupled to said memory means and to said input means for detecting and indentifying [sic] differences between said words and sentences [in the] first and second groups of said characters;
    display means coupled to said processing means for providing a display of said differences.

One might be concerned that any comparison program, past and future, would satisfy this description. Before passage of the Patent Act of 1952, which is our present law, claims written in this "means plus function" format were not permitted because of a previous U. S. Supreme Court case, *Halliburton Oil Well Cementing Co.* v. *Walker*. That case held that claims written in "means plus function" format were invalid. The court was concerned that such claims would cover any means for performing the specified functions, regardless of whether or not the means were equivalent to what was described in the patent. In 1952, Congress changed the patent law to overrule the Halliburton case and allow the patent owner to claim his invention in "means plus function" format. However, perhaps to alleviate the concern expressed in the Halliburton case, Congress expressly required in §112 that for there to be infringement the patent owner must show that the alleged infringer used the same means as described in the patent, or their equivalents: "An element in a claim for a combination may be expressed as a means or step for performing a specified function without the recital of structure, material, or acts in support thereof, and such claim shall be construed to cover the corresponding structure, material, or acts described in the specification and equivalents thereof."

Halliburton

Case: *Halliburton Oil Well Cementing Co.* v. *C. P. Walker*, 329 U.S. 1 (1946)

Date: December 18, 1946

Summary: Walker sued Halliburton Co. for infringement of his patent. The patent claimed an improvement on a method of measuring the distance from the ground down to the surface of the oil underground. A previous patent had been issued to Lehr and Wyatt for such measurement, but Walker had found a way to improve on their method to achieve greater accuracy. His claims in the patent did not spell out the physical embodiment of the improvement, but described it in terms of the required function.

Decision: The Supreme Court invalidated his claims, stating that they were too vague because they did not specify the physical requirements for the mechanism.

A more recent case underscored this interpretation of the 1952 law and made it clear that every one of the claimed functions had to be present in the challenged device before it could be found to be infringing. In *Pennwalt Corp.* v. *Durand-Wayland*, in which Pennwalt charged Durand-Wayland with infringing Pennwalt's patent, the Appeals Court found that: "The statute means exactly what it says: To determine whether a claim limitation is met literally, where expressed as a means for performing a stated function, the court must compare the accused structure *with the disclosed structure*, and must find equivalent *structure* as well as *identity* of claimed *function* for that structure."

The effect of this is to require that not only does a plaintiff have to show that an alleged infringer is solving the same problem in the same general way, it is also necessary to show that each of the sub-functions disclosed in the patent specification must be present (at least in an equivalent way) in the accused machine or process.

Pennwalt

Case: *Pennwalt Corp. v. Durand-Wayland, Inc.*, 833 F.2d 931 (Fed. Cir. 1987)

Date: November 6, 1987

Summary: Pennwalt sued Durand-Wayland for infringing its patent on a fruit sorter. The issue in the case was whether the District Court should have gone beyond "the means-plus-function language of a claim limitation [in the patent application in] comparing the structure in the accused devices with the *structure* disclosed in the specification."

Decision: The Appeals Court found that the District Court's opinion was not clearly erroneous; that is, some of the functions in the claimed inventions were in fact missing from the allegedly infringing machine, and therefore there was no infringement.

In a part of the ruling that will probably be quoted in future patent trials regarding computer devices, the Appeals Court also stated:

Pennwalt argues that the "accused machines simply do in a computer what the patent illustrates doing with hard-wired circuitry," and asserts that "this alone is insufficient to escape infringement." If Pennwalt was correct that the accused devices differ only in substituting a computer for hard-wired circuitry, it might have a stronger position for arguing that the accused devices infringe the claims. The claim limitations, however, require the performance of certain specified functions. Theoretically, a microprocessor could be programmed to perform those functions. However, the district court found that the microprocessor in the accused devices was not so programmed.

In that case, actual functions found in the Pennwalt fruit sorter were missing from the Durand-Wayland devices. If these functions had been there, and the only difference was a literal translation to a computer program of the particular implementation described in the specification, there might well have been a finding of infringement.

The impact on the software field of the Advanced Software text-comparing invention, then, appears to be to protect the specific means used in comparing documents and probably the specific method of displaying the differences within the context of the original documents. Because the method is described using sophisticated techniques such as hashing and the CPU interrupt mechanism, it is probable that methods not using these techniques are not subject to challenge. On the other hand, other inventors must find techniques for doing the comparisons that are as efficient as these, or at least work well enough, in order to compete in the market. That is fine, of course, and is consistent with the spirit of the Constitution's goal of "securing for limited Times to Authors and Inventors the exclusive Right to their respective Writings and Discoveries."

There may still be the question as to how broadly a specific technique, such as hashing, might be interpreted. Although the courts have traditionally interpreted claims of previous patents quite narrowly, thus giving a new inventor more leeway, the PTO has used a broader interpretation. The effect of this has been to reject some patent applications because the examiner has ruled that a previous patent's claims either anticipated the current invention, or made it obvious, in that the particular method described in the new one was somehow included in the broad interpretation of the claims of the earlier one.

In a 1994 case known as *In Re Donaldson*, the U. S. Court of Appeals for the Federal Circuit, which handles patent appeals, stated: "Our holding does not conflict with the principle that claims are to be given their 'broadest reasonable interpretation' during prosecution. . . . Rather, our holding in this case merely sets a limit on how broadly the PTO may construe means-plus-function language under the rubric of 'reasonable interpretation.' . . . One is still subject to the requirement that a claim 'particularly point out and distinctly claim' the invention. One must set forth an adequate disclosure showing what is meant by that language."

Because of the differing practices of the courts and the PTO in the past, the Appeals Court made a deliberate finding in that regard as well: "Because no distinction is made in [the statute] between prosecution in the PTO and enforcement in the courts, or between validity and infringement, we hold that [the statute] applies regardless of the context in which the interpretation of means-plus-function language arises, i.e.,

whether as part of a patentability determination in the PTO or as part of a
validity or infringement determination in a court."

It is not yet clear what this will mean in the operation of the PTO, but
the effect may be to encourage more patents to be issued with
incremental improvements over previous inventions.

Donaldson

Case: *In Re Donaldson Company, Inc.,*
         91-1386 (Reexamination Serial NO. 90/001,776), U. S.
         Court of Appeals for the Federal Circuit

Date: February 14, 1994

Original decision: January 30, 1991 (Board of Patent Appeals and
         Interferences), reaffirmed on April 17, 1991

Summary: Donaldson, assignee of the Schuler patent (#4,395,269) on a
         dust collector device, appealed a decision rejecting one of its
         claims. The basis of the rejection was that Schuler's claim
         was obvious in light of a previous patent (#3,421,295) by
         Smith, which also described a dust collector. Schuler's
         claim described a membrane that would respond to changes
         in air pressure, thus loosening dust which otherwise might
         resist being removed from the collector. Smith's dust
         collector did not include such a membrane, although there
         was a provision for carrying away the collected dust. The
         issue was how broadly the Smith patent claims should be
         interpreted, beyond the actual specification included in the
         Smith patent.

Decision: The decision was reversed, in favor of Donaldson. In other
         words, the PTO and the Board of Appeals had interpreted
         the Smith claim too broadly (beyond the specification), to
         include the invention of Schuler as an obvious extension.

NOTES

1. Appendix A of the CONTU report, p. 17
2. Emily Brower, "Software Patents Not Yet Tested," *MacWEEK*, April 18,
1989, p. 58

3.   The Supreme Court did continue to reject purely "mathematical algorithms." I will comment on this aspect in Chapter 11.

4.   The Tribune Company acquired Compton from Encyclopedia Britannica in September, 1993, and shares the patent with Encyclopedia Britannica.

5.   #5,241,671 "Multimedia Search System Using a Plurality of Entry Path Means which Indicate Interrelatedness of Information," filed October 26, 1989, issued August 31, 1993.

6.   December 14, 1993.

7.   Hashing is a technique for searching a database in which the search key is transformed into another form by a mathematical computation to facilitate and expedite the search. An interrupt is a mechanism usually used to signal an event whose timing is not predictable. A cursor is a pointing indicator on a screen, often manipulated by a mouse or by key strokes.

8.   It is unfortunate that the legal language used to state the claims seems to reflect the possibly medieval origins of patent law. One can only hope that our legal colleagues will some day find it possible to communicate more effectively with the rest of us, without any loss of the precision they clearly need in such documents.

4

The Tangible Medium

We now return to our discussion of copyright law. Section 101 of the 1976 Copyright Act, 17 U.S.C. §102, states in part: "(a) Copyright protection subsists . . . in original works of authorship fixed in any tangible medium of expression, now known or later developed, from which they can be perceived, reproduced, or otherwise communicated, either directly or with the aid of a machine or device. Works of authorship include the following categories: (1) literary works; . . . (6) motion pictures and other audiovisual works." (This was later amended to include sound recordings and architectural works.)

If you were a lawyer planning to defend a client against a charge of copyright infringement, how might you use Section 101 to show that there was no valid basis for copyright protection for the software the client was alleged to have copied? The two aspects that were especially appealing to lawyers in the early 1980s were the fixation requirement and the communication requirement. Fixation is defined in §101 as follows: "A work is 'fixed' in a tangible medium of expression when its embodiment in a copy or phonorecord, by or under the authority of the author, is sufficiently permanent or stable to permit it to be perceived, reproduced or otherwise communicated for a period of more than transitory duration."

The case that has been the basis for settling many of these issues in the computer field is *Williams Electronics, Inc.* v. *Artic Int'l, Inc.*, which concerned coin-operated video games.

Williams

Case: *Williams Electronics, Inc.* v. *Artic Int' l, Inc.*,
685 F.2d 870 (3rd Cir. 1982)

Date: August 2, 1982

Summary: Williams Electronics manufactures and sells coin-operated
electronic video games, including the DEFENDER. Artic
began to sell a kit that, when connected to a CRT display,
presents a game, DEFENSE COMMAND, which is almost
identical to DEFENDER. The District Court found that
Artic had infringed the Williams copyright on its computer
program and its audiovisual works. The defendant appealed.
The issues included: (1) whether the audiovisual copyrights
satisfy the requirement that the work be "fixed in any
tangible medium of expression," and (2) whether copyright
protection for source code extends to the object code
resulting from a translation of the source code.

Decision: The Appeals Court affirmed the decision of the District
Court in favor of Williams Electronics.

The DEFENDER game, marketed by Williams, was protected by three
copyright registrations, one covering the computer program, one
covering the audiovisual effects seen when the game was in the "attract"
mode (that is, when no one was playing, and the goal was to attract
someone to play), and one covering the audiovisual effects seen when
someone was in fact playing the game and interacting with the computer
program. Artic marketed a game that the Federal District Court found to
be "virtually identical" to the Williams game. As stated by the Appeals
Court, "the attract mode of the Artic game is substantially identical to
that of Williams' game, with minor exceptions such as the absence of the
Williams name and the substitution of the terms 'DEFENSE' and/or
'DEFENSE COMMAND' for the term 'DEFENDER' in its display."

In the appeal, Artic did not dispute the findings of the District Court
on copying, but instead argued against the scope and validity of the
copyright, and, therefore, the finding of infringement. In particular, Artic
claimed unsuccessfully that the images in the Williams game are

transient, that is, they cannot be "fixed." According to the Appeals Court:

Specifically, [Artic] contends that there is a lack of "fixation" because the video game generates or creates "new" images each time the attract mode or play mode is displayed, notwithstanding the fact that the new images are identical or substantially identical to the earlier ones.

We reject this contention. The fixation requirement is met whenever the work is "sufficiently permanent or stable to permit it to be . . . reproduced, or otherwise communicated" for more than a transitory period. Here the original audiovisual features of the DEFENDER game repeat themselves over and over.

Defendant also apparently contends that the player's participation withdraws the game's audiovisual work from copyright eligibility because there is no set or fixed performance and the player becomes a co-author of what appears on the screen. Although there is player interaction with the machine during the play mode which causes the audiovisual presentation to change in some respects from one game to the next in response to the player's varying participation, there is always a repetitive sequence of a substantial portion of the sights and sounds of the game, and many aspects of the display remain constant from game to game regardless of how the player operates the controls. . . . Furthermore, there is no player participation in the attract mode which is displayed repetitively without change.

We shall see later that there is still dispute over the extent of copyright protection to be afforded to screen presentations, but at least the Willams case appears to have settled the "tangible medium" and "fixation" questions with regard to screen displays.

Another issue raised by Artic International is the difference between "source" and "object" code with respect to copyright protection. Artic argued that object code cannot be protected because a copy must be intelligible to human beings and must be intended as a medium of communication to human beings. In an early case, a piano roll was not considered a copy of a musical composition because at most a few expert people could "perceive" it.[1] According to the Williams Appeals Court, however: "The answer to defendant's contention is in the words of the statute itself. A 'copy' is defined to include a material object in which a work is fixed 'by *any* method now known or later developed, and *from which the work can be perceived*, reproduced, or otherwise communicated, either directly or *with the aid of a machine or device*' (17 U.S.C. § 101) (emphasis added). We cannot accept defendant's suggestion that would afford an unlimited loophole by which infringement of a computer program is limited to copying of the computer program text but not to duplication of a computer program fixed on a silicon chip."

A year after the Appeals Court decision in the Williams case, an issue concerning the difference between operating systems and application programs was raised almost simultaneously in two cases: *Apple Computer, Inc.* v. *Formula Int'l, Inc.* and *Apple Computer, Inc.* v. *Franklin Computer Corporation.* Although these cases were filed in district courts located in different federal circuits, the Third Circuit and the Ninth Circuit, the two courts issued remarkably consistent opinions.

Formula

Case: *Apple Computer, Inc.* v. *Formula Int'l, Inc.,*
            725 F.2d 521 (9th Cir. 1984)

Date: February 8, 1984

Summary: Formula International sold a computer kit using the name "Pineapple," which was designed to be compatible with the Apple II computer manufactured by Apple Computer. In the ROM of the Pineapple computer were two programs that were admittedly substantially similar to two copyrighted Apple programs. The District Court granted a preliminary injunction to Apple, which Formula appealed. The issues included: (1) whether the programs controlled the internal operation of the computer, and hence were only ideas or processes, and therefore were not copyrightable, and (2) whether a computer program is protected by copyright only if it embodies expression that is communicated to the user when the program is run.

Decision: The Appeals Court affirmed the decision of the District Court.

In the Formula International case, the defendants, Formula International, claimed that so-called operating programs should not be copyrightable because they are intended to control the actions of the computer and are not like "application programs," which directly produce visual images or expressions to be viewed by humans. They argued that an operating program is an "idea" or a "method of operation" or a "system" (using the language of the Copyright Act — Section 102(b) — that excludes from copyright protection "any idea, procedure, process, system, method of operation, concept, principle, or discovery"). It is interesting that to support this argument they presented the court with uses of these words by various computer practitioners. However, the judge rejected this argument because the people quoted would have had no idea of the legal interpretations of their choice of words.

The very clear statement of the judge in the Formula case that settled this particular issue was:

Essentially, all computer programs as embodied in ROMs and diskettes are designed to operate a machine in such a way as to ultimately produce some useful communication to the user — that is their purpose. It is difficult to understand how they can be classified into two categories for copyright purposes, with protection afforded to one category and not the other, based on whether they directly generate that communication or whether they merely direct certain machine functions which eventually result in that expression. Either all computer programs so embodied are within the terms "idea, procedure, system, method of operation" and are excluded, or all of them are outside those terms and thus protectable. There is nothing in any of the statutory terms which suggests a different result for different types of computer programs based upon the function they serve within the machine.

Again with regard to the argument that object code did not warrant copyright protection, the Appeals Court in the Franklin case further affirmed the copyrightability of object code by relating it to the definition of a computer program: "The definition of 'computer program' adopted by Congress in the 1980 amendments is 'sets of statements or instructions to be used *directly or indirectly* in a computer in order to bring about a certain result (17 U.S.C. §101) (emphasis added). As source code instructions must be translated into object code before the computer can act upon them, only instructions expressed in object code can be used "directly" by the computer."

The clear implication here is that because the National Commission on New Technological Uses of Copyrighted Works report clearly recommended that object code be copyrightable, and because the amendment referred to came after that recommendation and was intended to be consonant with the National Commission on New Technological Uses of Copyrighted Works report, the definition of "computer program" was not to be used to distinguish between source code and object code.

Franklin

Case: *Apple Computer, Inc.* v. *Franklin Computer Corp.,*
714 F.2d 1240 (3rd Cir. 1983), cert. dismissed 464 U. S.
1033 (1984)

Date: August 30, 1983

Summary: Apple Computer marketed a successful computer, the Apple
II. Franklin Computer then marketed a computer, the ACE
100, designed to be compatible with the Apple II. Franklin
admitted copying much of the operating system written by
Apple for the Apple II, but contended that it was not feasible
for them to write their own operating system to be
compatible with the Apple hardware. They challenged the
Apple copyright and raised several issues: (1) whether
copyright protection extends to object code, (2) whether
code embedded in ROM can be copyrighted, and (3)
whether an operating system can be copyrighted. The
District Court denied a motion for a preliminary injunction
because there was "some doubt as to the copyrightability of
the programs."

Decision: The Appeals Court reversed the denial of the preliminary
injunction, and remanded the case back to the District Court.

A further issue in the Williams case, and again in the Franklin case,
was whether object code embedded in ROM, and hence in some sense a
part of the physical machine, could be copyrighted. This was clearly
established in the affirmative in the Appeals Court opinion in the
Franklin case:

Just as the district court's suggestion of a distinction between source code and
object code was rejected by our opinion in *Williams* . . . so also was its
suggestion that embodiment of a computer program on a ROM, as
distinguished from in a traditional writing, detracts from its copyrightability. In
Williams we rejected the argument that "a computer program is not infringed
when the program is loaded into electronic memory devices (ROMs) and used
to control the activity of machines." . . . Defendant there had argued that there
can be no copyright protection for the ROMs because they are utilitarian
objects or machine parts. We held that the statutory requirement of "fixation,"
the manner in which the issue arises, is satisfied through the embodiment of

the expression in the ROM devices. Therefore we reaffirm that a computer program in object code embedded in a ROM chip is an appropriate subject of copyright.

The Franklin case was heard by the usual Appeals Court in the Third Circuit. Franklin's request for another hearing by the Appeals Court "En Banc," which consists of a much larger number of judges than the usual panel of three, was turned down. The issues decided there appear to be firmly decided. Of course, other lawsuits on other issues continue to be filed, as the ramifications of the application of copyright protection to software become more apparent and more complicated.

An interesting twist in the application of these results occurred in the Intel trial, when NEC argued that Intel's microcode did not satisfy the definition of "computer program," and, hence, was not software and was not copyrightable, because, as reported in the court's opinion while rejecting that argument: "it cannot be used *in* a computer and also be a defining part of the computer." (See Appendix A for more information on microcode.) The opinion continued: "But, as stated at the outset, Intel's microcode is within the statutory definition of a 'computer program,' and NEC's semi-semantical argument runs counter to the authority cited by Intel: 'There is nothing in any of the statutory terms which suggests a different result [concerning copyrightability] for different types of computer programs based upon the function they serve within the machine.'"[2]

NOTES

1.   White-Smith Music Publishing Co. v. Apollo Co., 209 U.S. 1, 28 S.Ct. 319, 52 L.Ed. 655 (1908).
2.   This is a quote from the Franklin opinion, quoting in turn from the Formula opinion.

5

Validity and Scope

It is not very often that someone is caught red-handed in the act of illegally copying software. Usually, all one has is a suspicion that some other product looks or behaves suspiciously like another, or that a competitive product could not possibly have been produced so quickly without copying at least some protected aspects of another product without permission. It is usually not easy to prove that impermissible copying has occurred, but every once in a while, the evidence is so clear that the defendant simply has to admit it. In such cases, what defenses are still available to a charge of copyright infringement?

One method that has been used in copyright defense is to argue that the copyright should not have been issued at all for that particular software. This argument has been rejected by the courts. Copyright registration is quite straightforward, and the Library of Congress, in which the Copyright Office resides, does not attempt to reject such registrations on substantive grounds. Another argument that has been used is that the "copyright notice" (that is, the symbol, ©, the year of publication, and the name of the copyright holder), sometimes referred to as the "copyright marker," had not been visible on the product. The inference is that the author did not actively try to protect the copyright from infringement, or that the alleged infringer might not have been aware of the copyright.

Until recently, that was one possible argument, actually used successfully by NEC in the Intel case. Although Intel had placed the notice on all of the computer chips they themselves produced, NEC and two other companies licensed by Intel to produce the same chips had manufactured and distributed millions of chips without the notice. Intel was apparently so slow to recognize this and to take appropriate remedial action, that the court found, at least partly for that reason, that the Intel copyright was no longer valid. The reasoning here was that a company lost all of its copyright protection if its copyright notice was not visible to the user.

In 1988 the United States adopted the Berne Copyright Convention generally observed in other countries. Among other provisions, under that convention one need not display the standard copyright notice for a work to be protected. Now an original work that otherwise qualifies for copyright protection does not lose that protection merely because the author has not placed a copyright notice on the work.[1]

Although the 1988 amendments to the Copyright Act would have helped Intel somewhat, it was primarily the merger argument that supported NEC's case for invalidation of the Intel copyright. How did the merger argument apply there? The Copyright Act explicitly stated: "In no case does copyright protection for an original work of authorship extend to any idea, procedure, process, system, method of operation, concept, principle, or discovery, regardless of the form in which it is described, explained, illustrated, or embodied in such work."[2] The merger argument asserts that if there is only one way, or a few ways, to express an idea, then one cannot copyright the expression, because that would grant protection — and, therefore, a monopoly — to the idea itself. As we have seen, NEC successfully argued that there were very few ways in which to write the microcode for its computer, given the hardware base used, and, thus, because of the merger argument, the Intel copyright should not have been issued.

Another way to argue that an original work should not have been issued a copyright is to claim that the work does not belong to any of the types of works listed in the Copyright Act as qualifying for protection. The Copyright Act states: "Works of authorship include the following categories: (1) Literary works; (2) musical works, including any accompanying words; (3) dramatic works, including any accompanying music; (4) pantomimes and choreographic works; (5) pictorial, graphic, and sculptural works; (6) motion pictures and other audiovisual works; (7) sound recordings, and (8) architectural works."[3] Each of the categories was further defined in the act, so that, for example: "'Literary works' are works, other than audiovisual works, expressed in words, numbers, or other verbal or numerical symbols or indicia, regardless of the nature of the material objects such as books, periodicals, manuscripts, phonorecords, film, tapes, disks, or cards, in which they are embodied."[4]

It was clear from the legislative history, moreover, that the list of eight categories was not intended to be exhaustive, but illustrative, and courts have since extended protection to televised news reports, blank answer sheets for student achievement tests and intelligence tests that would be corrected by optical scanning devices, and other works which did not exactly fit the list spelled out in the Copyright Act.

With all of this specificity, the court must still determine in each case whether a particular example of work intended to be used within a computer would be included in one of the categories defined in the Copyright Act. That was exactly the question in the Allen-Myland case.

Allen-Myland

Case: *Allen-Myland, Inc.* v. *IBM*,
              770 F.Supp. 1004, 1014 (E.D.Pa. 1991)

Date: August 1, 1991

Original decision: 746 F.Supp. 520 (E.D.Pa. 1990)

Summary: Allen-Myland (AMI) was charged with copyright infringe-
              ment by IBM (after AMI had charged IBM with violating
              the Sherman Antitrust Act). AMI had made copies of part of
              the information needed to properly reconfigure large
              mainframe systems. They had also created new versions of
              this information by combining portions of the originals,
              which they then used in reconfiguring systems. Some of
              these new versions did not work properly in customers'
              systems.

Decision: AMI was found to have infringed IBM's copyright, and was
              ordered to cease making new copies. Certain questions of
              implementation of the injunctive relief decision were dele-
              gated to a Special Master for a recommendation.

In order for IBM to monitor the performance of, and provide maintenance for, its large computers in the series called "the 3090 family," a second, smaller computer, the Processor Controller, continuously obtains information from the 3090 system while it is computing, and analyzes that information to make sure that everything is working properly. If there is a sign that some part of the computer is malfunctioning or overheating, or any other indication that some component of the extremely complex 3090 computer system is behaving in an unusual way, the Processor Controller determines which part seems to be causing trouble. It then "calls home," that is, it establishes a telephone connection with another computer at an IBM plant in New York and reports the problem to a program in that computer. Based on a sophisticated analysis involving both the Processor Controller and the computer in New York, an order is placed for service personnel to initiate a repair trip to the affected 3090 system. The service people are even supplied with detailed instructions on the repair to be done, to the point of specifying which replacement parts are to be taken to the site.

The software on the Processor Controller, normally provided on five magnetic tapes, was the issue in the trial. AMI is in the business of changing various components and features; that is, reconfiguring various models of the 3090 to transform them into other models, as requested by customers. For example, one system might have 32 "channels," used to communicate with input/output (I/O) devices, while another might have 64. One system might have 128 million bytes of primary storage, and another might have 64 million bytes. One system might have two processors, another four, and so on.

AMI's primary customers are third-party leasing companies, whose business is mainly buying new large mainframe computers, primarily from IBM, and leasing them to end users; that is, companies that find it best to lease large computers, rather than buy them. One of the reasons why leasing is a good idea for some users is that as their needs change, they can ask the leasing company to reconfigure the system appropriately.[5] When a leasing company needs to reconfigure a system for a customer, or remove a system and lease it to another customer with different needs, it generally calls upon AMI or one of AMI's competitors (sometimes IBM itself) to do the reconfiguring job. Once the system has been reconfigured, a new set of tapes is needed for the Processor Controller, to reflect the new configuration. Because more than 80,000 different configurations are possible, with each new configuration based on a different set of components and features, it is necessary to create new Processor Controller information tapes for each combination. The Processor Controller needs precise information as to the structure and organization of the particular 3090 whose performance it is monitoring because that is the input into the analysis necessary when it calls home to report a problem. In many reconfigurations, only Tape 2 needs to be changed, and therefore only that tape must be replaced, but in some cases all five of the tapes must be changed.

IBM discovered that AMI had made copies of Processor Controller information that had come its way, and had created a library of such copies, primarily of copies of Tape 2. IBM brought suit against AMI. According to the amended Copyright Act in 1980:

It is not an infringement for the owner of a copy of a computer program to make or authorize the making of another copy or adaptation of that computer program provided:

(1) that such a new copy or adaptation is created as an essential step in the utilization of the computer program in conjunction with a machine and that it is used in no other manner, or

(2) that such new copy or adaptation is for archival purposes only and that all archival copies are destroyed in the event that continued possession of the computer program should cease to be rightful.

Any exact copies prepared in accordance with the provisions of this section may be leased, sold, or otherwise transferred, along with the copy from which such copies were prepared, only as part of the lease, sale, or other transfer of all rights in the program. Adaptations so prepared may be transferred only with the authorization of the copyright owner.[6]

Although AMI claimed during the trial that copies of the various versions of Tape 2 were archival copies, IBM charged that AMI was not entitled to make and keep such copies, under the provisions of the Copyright Act just quoted. In some cases, such as for systems actually still owned by IBM, no permission was given at all to make a copy. In other cases, there may have been permission from a third-party leasing company to make a copy, and even to adapt it for the new configuration that AMI was putting together. However, there could not have been permis-sion for AMI to have kept a copy of the tape in its library once the computer system was shipped out to the end user. There were other complicated arguments, but the case finally came down to the defense's argument that the information on Tape 2 should not have been copyrightable at all.

The basis for the alleged non-copyrightable nature of Tape 2 was that, because it consisted of "mere configuration data," it was not a literary work, or any other kind of work that qualifies for copyright protection. AMI was arguing that the information on Tape 2 was just a list of numbers or other data that identified the components of the particular computer system being described. IBM argued that the information on the tape was not just a list of values. Rather, there were a number of distinguishable files on the tape, and several of them contained actual program information. The form of the files that IBM claimed were program information was quite important. In those cases, there were program modules, or subroutines, on another tape, usually Tape 1, that were "called," or invoked, by sequences of commands on Tape 2. IBM's argument, therefore, was that the commands on Tape 2 really controlled the sequence of actions — each of which was programmed in detail on Tape 1 — that responded to signals from the 3090 computer system under various circumstances, some normal, and some abnormal. Thus, the information on Tape 2 was an integral part of the software for the Processor Controller, and hence was copyrightable.

Another case involving third-party rights under copyright law is *MAI Systems Corp.* v. *Peak Computer, Inc.* In this case, which may have far-reaching consequences, Peak was providing computer maintenance service to its clients, many of whom used MAI computers and software. MAI also provides service to many of its customers, and undertook action against Peak for copyright infringement. According to the court opinion, the software licenses which bound MAI customers "do not allow for the use or copying of MAI software by third parties such as Peak. Therefore, any 'copying' done by Peak is 'beyond the scope' of the license."

The importance of this case lies in the interpretation by the court that

"copying" for purposes of copyright law occurs when a computer program is transferred from a permanent storage device to a computer's RAM. . . . The loading of copyrighted computer software from a storage medium . . . into the memory of a central processing unit ("CPU") causes a copy to be made. . . . Peak argues that this loading of copyrighted software does not constitute a copyright violation because the "copy" created in RAM is not "fixed." . . . We find no specific facts (and Peak points to none) which indicate that the copy created in the RAM is not fixed.

The court permanently enjoined Peak from further infringing MAI's software copyright, which means that Peak would have to get its own license from MAI in order to service any MAI equipment for a third party. Just the act of turning on the computer and causing the operating system to be loaded was judged to be copyright infringement. Presumably, Peak could have the customer operate the computer while servicing it, but that would be an awkward situation in any case.

The finding of the Peak court may have even more far-reaching effects. A person acting as a consultant or educator would have to think twice before using a computer on someone else's premises to demonstrate something. According to the Peak decision, any act of loading an operating system or an application program might under some circumstances be construed as copyright violation. It may be hoped that future cases will limit the effects of this decision.

Peak

Case: *MAI Systems Corp.* v. *Peak Computer, Inc.,* 991 F.2d 511 (9th Cir. 1993)

Date: April 7, 1993

Original decision: No. 92-55363 (C. D. Cal 1992)

Summary: MAI used to manufacture computers and designed software for those systems. Now it continues to service its computers and software. Peak also services computers and software, and many of its customers have MAI systems. MAI charged that Peak was violating MAI's software copyright by making copies of the software in loading it into the computer while providing maintenance service. The customer license for the software did not authorize a third party to make copies. Peak argued that the copy made by loading the software into the main memory was not "fixed".

Decision: The District Court, affirmed by the Appeals Court, permanently enjoined Peak from using MAI software without its own license. The license of the Peak customer did not extend to a third party.

One argument that IBM might have used in the AMI case, but did not, is that the information on Tape 2 was a compilation of information. Not every compilation is protected under the Copyright Act, but the general category of compilations is covered. In §101 a "compilation" is defined for copyright purposes as "a work formed by the collection and assembly of preexisting materials or of data that are selected, coordinated, or arranged in such a way that the resulting work as a whole constitutes an original work of authorship." On the other hand, §103(b) contains a rather severe limitation on the protection of compilations: "The copyright in a compilation . . . extends only to the material contributed by the author of such work, as distinguished from the preexisting material employed in the work, and does not imply any exclusive right in the preexisting material."

In the Allen-Myland case, much of the material on the tape in question was clearly original with IBM, but for its own reasons this was not the argument IBM chose to use in the litigation.

The 1991 Feist decision by the Supreme Court brought the compilation aspect of copyright law into sharp focus, however. Plaintiff Rural Telephone produced a directory with "white pages" and "yellow pages" covering the area it served, as do most telephone companies. Defendant Feist Publications specialized in wide-area directories, and it undertook to produce and market a directory covering a much larger region. To do so, it needed to use information most easily available from the directories generated by the 11 telephone companies in that larger region, one of which was Rural Telephone. Feist obtained licenses from the other 10 telephone companies to use the information in their directories, but Rural refused to license Feist for that purpose. As noted in the Supreme Court's opinion: "Feist and Rural compete vigorously for yellow pages advertising," and one may assume that Rural was not anxious to make the job easier for Feist.

Feist

Case: *Feist Publications, Inc.* v. *Rural Telephone Service Co., Inc.*,
            499 U.S. 340 (1991)

Date: March 27, 1991

Original decision: 663 F.Supp. 214 (Kan., 1987), 737 F.Supp. 610 (Kan. 1990), 916 F.2d 718 (10th Cir. 1990)

Summary: Feist Publications wanted to publish a telephone directory (white pages) for a region covering 11 different telephone service areas, and tried to obtain licenses from the various telephone companies to use the data in the directories that they were mandated to publish by state law. Rural refused to grant a license for this purpose. Feist went ahead and used Rural's listings. Rural sued, claiming copyright infringement.

Decision: The District Court's decision granting summary judgement to Rural (and affirmed by the Appeals Court) was reversed. The Supreme Court held that there was nothing original in Rural's selection and arrangement of the information contained in the white pages, and that original authorship is a prerequisite to copyrightable subject matter. The opinion also rejected the "sweat of the brow" argument based on the amount of effort that Rural had invested in creating their publication.

A directory produced by Feist without listings for the area covered by Rural would have been seriously deficient. Therefore, Feist resorted to using about 1,300 entries from Rural's 1982–83 white pages. Feist employees did verify the information, and they added new information, such as street addresses, which Rural did not provide. The Feist employees also used four fictitious listings, which Rural, like many list maintainers, had included in its directory to detect unauthorized use of their data. There was little doubt, therefore, that there had been copying of the Rural data.

Rural sued Feist for copyright infringement, arguing that its data was protected as part of its compilation. Feist argued that going door-to-door, or even telephoning everyone, to obtain the same information, was economically impractical. Besides, Feist said, the scope of the copyright protection did not include the facts in the directory. Feist argued that Rural could not claim protection for the pre-existing material represented by the names, towns, and telephone numbers listed in the directory.

A number of previous cases reviewed in the Feist opinion had clearly established that originality can be introduced into compilations in the selection and arrangement of material, even if the material itself comes from the public domain. This case came down to the questions of whether Rural had demonstrated an original selection and arrangement of its facts, that is, of the individual entries in its directory, and whether Feist had thereby violated its copyright. The court's clearly written opinion gave the basic principle involved: "Copyright treats facts and factual compilations in a wholly consistent manner. Facts, whether alone or as part of a compilation, are not original and therefore may not be copyrighted. A factual compilation is eligible for copyright if it features an original selection or arrangement of facts, but the copyright is limited to the particular selection or arrangement. In no event may copyright extend to the facts themselves."

An interesting section of the court's opinion in this case reviewed the history of these questions. It seems quite reasonable that the scope of copyright protection should not extend to facts just because those facts are included in someone's compilation, unless there was some originality in their selection. But there were, apparently, some lower courts during the 1920s and 1930s for which it was not so clear. Referring to these courts as "sweat of the brow" courts, the Feist opinion quotes a 1922 opinion[7]: "The right to copyright a book upon which one has expended labor in its preparation does not depend upon whether the materials which he has collected consist or not of matters which are publici juris, or whether such materials show literary skill or originality, either in thought or in language, or anything more than industrious collection. The man who goes through the streets of a town and puts down the names of each of the inhabitants, with their occupations and their street number, acquires material of which he is the author."[8]

The only way to get around this total control of the facts involved would have been to go out and do all of the ground work again. Needless to say, this led to some confusion, with some courts applying the sweat of the brow criterion and some deciding that the facts were public and could not be protected, even in a copyrighted work. In the 1976 Copyright Act, Congress remedied that aspect of the law, based on a recommendation from the Copyright Office. The earlier phrase: "all the writings of an author" was replaced by: "original works of authorship," with the legislative history making it clear that Congress did not view this change as making new law, but clarifying what had been the law all along, even though some courts had misinterpreted it at times.

Having, thus, asserted that the facts that Feist copied were not protected, the court considered whether Feist had copied anything of the selection and arrangement of the data that might have been original with Rural. With regard to selection, it was pointed out that Kansas state law required the publication of the names and telephone numbers as part of Rural's monopoly franchise, and that "Rural expended sufficient effort to make the white pages directory useful, but insufficient creativity to make it original." The court also pointed out that "there is nothing remotely creative about arranging names alphabetically in a white pages directory. It is an age-old practice, firmly rooted in tradition and so commonplace that it has come to be expected as a matter of course." The court, therefore, concluded that Rural had no copyright in the white pages of the telephone directory.

It is interesting to note that some white pages directories have recently arranged their presentation of names somewhat differently. In at least one available directory names are arranged alphabetically, but presented without the repetition of the surname:

JONES,
> Robert ...
> Samuel ...
> Troy ...
> Zeke ...

One could ask whether this presentation would have made a difference in the Feist case. The probable answer is that if Feist had used the same format to present its data, there might have been copyright infringement, because the presentation format would represent an original arrangement of the data, but if Feist merely copied the data and presented it in some other format, there would not have been infringement. On the other hand, one might argue that there are so few ways to present alphabetized names that to allow any copyright protection would merge the idea and the expression, so even the arrangement shown above should not be protected.

NOTES

1.   The copyright does not even have to be registered with the Copyright Office before it can be infringed. In other words, because protection begins with creation of the work, infringement can occur at any time after that. On the other hand, registration is a prerequisite to filing an infringement action (17 U.S.C. §411), and neither statutory damages nor attorneys' fees are recoverable for any period prior to registration (unless registration is effected within three months after first publication) (17 U.S.C. §412).

2.   17 U. S. C. §102(b) (1980).

3.   17 U. S. C. §102(a) (1988).

4.   17 U. S. C. §101 (1980).

5.   Of course, financial arrangements are often the primary reason for leasing, but reconfiguration may be a concern as well.

6.   17 U. S. C. §117 (1980).

7.   *Jeweler's Circular Publ. Co.* v. *Keystone Publ. Co.*, 281 F. 83 (CA2 1922).

8.   When something is owned by the general public, such as air and light, it is referred to as *publici juris*.

6

Infringement

Webster's dictionary[1] defines "infringement" as "encroaching or trespassing on the rights of others." Given the exclusive, but limited, rights reserved to copyright holders in the Copyright Act, infringement would be actions that violate those rights without permission, subject to the exceptions that limit those rights.

According to the National Commission on New Technological Uses of Copyrighted Works report, "One is always free to make the machine do the same thing as it would if it had the copyrighted work placed in it, but only by one's own creative effort rather than by piracy." That is fine, but how does one prove piracy — that is, illegal copying of all or part of someone else's work? How does one prove that someone has infringed a copyright?

The easiest way is to catch the person in the act, but of course that almost never happens. There have been cases, however, where the evidence of copying has been pretty convincing. The Williams opinion finds:

(1) The game . . . contains an error which was present in early versions of the Williams computer program.

(2) The attract mode of both games displays a listing of high scores achieved by previous players alongside their initials, and Artic's game contains the initials of Williams employees, including its president, who initially achieved the highest scores.

. . .

(4) The Williams program provided that the words "Copyright 1980 — Williams Electronics" in code were to be stored in its memory . . . a "buried" or hidden copyright notice. . . . The listings [of the Artic memory] contained the "buried Williams copyright notice."

In another case, I was shown octal "dumps," that is, printouts, of portions of the memory from computers containing two vendors' operating systems. Overlaying the transparencies of the two printouts showed that the only difference between them in one section was the small area in one that contained blanks, where the original had stored the characters "© Copyright," including the date and the name of the company.

Another example is found in the Broderbund case. Testimony disclosed that the Unison programmers involved in the case were actually told to copy Broderbund's program, but they did so rather carelessly. As evidence of this, the court noted that in the original (Broderbund) program the user at one point is instructed to press the return key on the Apple keyboard associated with the computer on which it ran. In the Unison version of the program, the user is similarly instructed to press the return key, except that the IBM keyboard being used for that program had an enter key and no return key. It was actually admitted during the trial that this error was due to the "programmer's intense concentration on copying" the Broderbund program.

Sometimes a copier will reproduce something from an original program or document that seems strange, and whose function is not clear. The copier is afraid that the item does in fact serve some purpose, and it might be dangerous to leave it out. Some authors include such hidden markers on purpose if they are worried about future copying, just as suppliers of mailing lists include fictitious names and addresses to catch illegal copying.[2] More often such situations occur simply because either "hooks" are included to which to attach future enhancements, or a vestigial name, number, or other artifact is inadvertently left behind when it should have been deleted.

An example of the latter occurred in the SAS Institute case, described in Chapter 2. A special command had been included in the SAS Institute program, undocumented in any user manual or otherwise made available outside the SAS Institute. This command could be invoked if needed to perform a particular statistical analysis on performance data collected during execution of the program. This option was later deleted, except for one overlooked reference to the name of the command. A completely functionless occurrence of the name of that command was later found in the S & H program, in a place exactly analogous to that of the overlooked reference in the SAS Institute program. As stated in the court's opinion, S & H admitted during the trial that "it specifically sought out, through the use of computer programs specifically prepared by S & H for this purpose, each such undocumented option or other feature . . . [which was] then carefully and precisely reproduced in the S & H code."

Such obvious, usually inadvertent errors are referred to as "smoking guns" because they are reminiscent of catching someone just after a shooting occurs, with the gun still smoking. The reason they are so convincing in litigation is that programmers have so many choices at every stage of their work. Experience has shown that people working independently to create computer programs have so many ways to organize the solutions to their problems, to design the user interface, and to select the specific machine instructions to be executed that even among a large number of programmers it is highly unlikely that one will find more than the most superficial similarities between the work of any two of them who have worked independently.

This is also one reason why in an academic setting it is relatively easy to recognize when students have collaborated more than they should have on a programming assignment. For example, in a recent case three students had identical grammatical errors in corresponding comments buried in their programs. There are absolutely no constraints in typical higher-level languages as to what may be written in a comment, or for that matter when and where to insert comments, yet the students included the same grammatically incorrect wording in each of their programs.

The more difficult case of proving copyright infringement occurs when there is no admitted copying and no obvious smoking guns. If there are enough similarities in the programs or the user interfaces, the suspicion is raised of non-independent development, if not direct copying, but how would that be proven in court?

As is often the case, the courts have not settled the issue of similarity completely. The main outline of the process is fairly clear, but there have been different rulings in different parts of the country. This can happen because in the federal court system a case is heard first in a District Court, whose decision may then be appealed to the Appeals Court in the appropriate one of twelve circuits, or regions. An Appeals Court decision, or a method of argument, in one such circuit then sets a precedent for that circuit, but this is not binding on another circuit, where a different precedent may be set on the same issue. When such a difference does arise, it remains for the Supreme Court to resolve it, and then this becomes the law or procedure for the country as a whole. In the next chapter, we shall see how this has affected the copyright litigation process, although we are fortunate that the problem discussed there has not been very significant for computer copyright cases, at least to date.

One standard reference for arguing copyright infringement is *Roth Greeting Cards* v. *United Card Co.* This case clearly spelled out that copying may be established or at least inferred by showing that the accused party had access to the original work, and that there is substantial similarity between the works in question. That seems reasonable, until it must be decided what "access" means, and what "substantial similarity" means. There usually is not much argument over access. Either the accused saw or otherwise knew about the original work or he or she did not know about it. One can argue about the level of detail that was available, and for how long it was available, to determine the degree of influence, but normally it is not too hard to prove access. As discussed in Chapter 10, however, it is possible to use a "clean-room procedure" to develop a new product, to try to insure that the access part of the argument fails. The whole discussion of similarities in order to establish copying is irrelevant if no access is proven.

Roth

Case: *Roth Greeting Cards* v. *United Card Co.*,
             429 F.2d 1106 (9th Cir. 1970)

Date: July 10, 1970

Summary: Roth Greeting Cards asked for an injunction against United
             Card's marketing of greeting cards that were similar to
             theirs. The trial court found for the defendant and declined
             to issue the injunction. Roth appealed. The issues included:
             (1) how much originality is needed beyond creation of the
             work, (2) whether the work should be considered as a whole
             for copyright protection, and not just the textual material,
             which was not necessarily original, and (3) whether the
             "total concept and feel" of the work can be the basis of
             copyright infringement.

Decision: The Appeals Court reversed the lower court's decision and
             remanded the case back to the District Court for further
             proceedings.

The one aspect in which the degree of access potentially makes some difference, is in the determination of what is substantially similar. As in the Krofft case to be considered in more detail in Chapter 7, some courts have used a so-called "Inverse Ratio Rule": "Since a very high degree of similarity is required in order to dispense with proof of access, it must logically follow that where proof of access is offered, the required degree of similarity may be somewhat less than would be necessary in the absence of such proof."

In other words, if there had been direct access over a long period of time, a smaller amount of similarity would suffice than otherwise might be the case. It would seem, however, to depend a great deal on the quality of the access, such as whether the alleged infringer had a real opportunity to copy the original product, or was forced to retain a great deal of information mentally for some period of time.

CHANGING A COPIED WORK
TO AVOID INFRINGEMENT

We shall return to the important question of establishing substantial similarity in Chapter 7. Here a different question is addressed: Can an alleged copier avoid a charge of copyright infringement by changing the resulting work so that it is no longer similar enough to the original work to support an infringement claim? Consider the following scenario.

A person named K. has access to some code belonging to Company Y, which has a valid copyright on the code. Company Y discovers that Company Z, for which K. works, has begun to market a product which is suspiciously like their own. Litigation follows, and in the course of "discovery" (the pre-trial exchange of information) Y's lawyers find that an earlier version of Z's product, Version 0, even has some smoking guns leading them to believe strongly that K. copied a great deal of Y's code. The current Version 2 of Z's product, which raised the suspicion in the first place, lacks the smoking guns because it has evolved from Version 0, and a number of changes and improvements have been made in the interim period. During the course of the litigation, Y's lawyers argue that the very strong evidence of copying available for Version 0 should suffice to establish copying, even though Version 2 is the currently marketed product. What would you decide?

There is a partial answer in the Altai case. In that case, the defendant, Altai, admitted copying, but they argued that they had set up a "clean room" to remedy the copying when it was discovered within their company.[3] By means of the clean room, they created non-infringing code that replaced the copied code. They argued that the product they then marketed did not infringe the original work. The court decided that the admitted copying affected sales of the original work prior to the removal of the copied portion, and thus affected the award of damages, but that in the future, no further damages were justified. (The infringing company also replaced the copied part with the results of their own work at all of their customers' sites.) This conclusion would not necessarily hold in all such cases, however. If the product of Altai, the defendant, had been so successful that it had taken over the market for that particular product, one might have been able to argue lasting damage to Computer Associates well into the future. The computation of damages is a very complex process, generally requiring the participation of expert economists, and it is often interesting to observe the different conclusions they reach in a given case.

Another example, which actually suggested the hypothetical example of K. above, was highlighted in the Intel case. Intel (Company Y) presented what it thought was good evidence that someone (K.) had copied some of its microcode directly into Version 0, but the court found that "there remains no basis for a claim of copying or even of substantial similarity,"[4] because enough changes had been made in Version 2. One would think that it would be better to determine whether copying had occurred by taking the evolution from Version 0 to Version 2 into account, if indeed copying could be established with respect to Version 0, but that does not seem to be the way the court approached it.

MERGER REVISITED

We have seen that the merger argument is one possible defense in copyright litigation. This is the argument that there is merging of the idea and the expression when there are very few expressive alternatives, leading to the possibility that granting a copyright would give its holder control of the idea. The question has arisen, however, as to when in the legal analysis the merger argument should be applied. If it is decided that the expression and the idea have merged, should that preclude the granting of a valid copyright? Or should the copyright be considered valid if all other conditions, such as original authorship, are established, with the merger argument being applied to the question of whether infringement has occurred?

On the one hand, it could be argued that the proper conclusion to be reached once the merger of idea and expression has been established is that there should be no valid copyright for at least that part of the program. Admittedly, it would be impossible, given the volume of copy-right applications, for the Copyright Office to discover such a situation at the time the copyright application was submitted for registration, but one should be able to argue later against the copyrightability of an expression if it leads directly to control of the idea. On the other hand, attempts have been made, using piecemeal arguments of this kind, to label individual elements of a program as unprotectable, in an attempt to avoid the court's reaching the question whether there was copying or not. Any literary work could be, thus, disadvantaged if such an argument could be made, because, ultimately, each such work is composed of letters, words, and ideas, all of which are individually unprotectable.

The courts seem to have adopted the latter point of view in some important cases. In the Intel case, the court states: "Although Ninth Circuit cases have not specifically discussed this [merger] issue raised by NEC, they appear uniformly to treat the 'merger' issue as a question of whether or not there is infringement rather than copyrightability."[5] The opinion goes on to argue that: "The Register of Copyrights will not know about the presence or absence of constraints that limit ways to express an idea. The burden of showing such constraints should be left to the alleged infringer. Accordingly, . . . the relationship between 'idea' and 'expression' will not be considered on the issue of copyrightability, but will be deferred to the discussion of infringement."

As we have already seen, the court determined in that case that there was indeed a merger of idea and expression, which greatly limited the Intel argument of infringement.

Another example of the use of the merger argument in the infringement context is the Summary Judgement action in the case of *Frybarger* v. *IBM, Inc.* In this case, Frybarger had developed a video game while employed by Gebelli, and Gebelli had allegedly used ele-ments of Frybarger's game in developing his own game. Gebelli had an agreement with IBM under which IBM would market his game, and Frybarger sued on the basis of copyright infringement. The District Court granted IBM and Gebelli a summary judgement, terminating the case, and it was appealed to the Ninth Circuit. The merger argument was central in this case, in that the Appeals Court concluded: "Although there are numerous similar features in Frybarger's and Gebelli's works, we believe that each of the similar features constitutes a basic idea of the videogames and, to the extent that each feature is expressive, that the expression is 'as a practical matter indispensable, or at least standard, in the treatment of a given [idea].'"

Frybarger

Case: *Frybarger* v. *International Business Machines Corporation*, 812 F.2d 525 (9th Cir. 1987)

Date: March 10, 1987

Summary: Frybarger had created a game, Tricky Trapper, while employed by Nasir Gebelli. Gebelli declined to market that game, but later entered into an agreement with IBM to market a game of his own, Mouser. Frybarger claimed that IBM (and Gebelli) had infringed on his copyright for Tricky Trapper. The issues involved the distinction between the idea and its expression, and whether the similarities between the two games were similarities of ideas only.

Decision: The court opinion, affirmed by the Appeals Court, held that those similarities that existed were at the level of ideas and general concepts, and that the expressions of those ideas were indispensable to the ideas. Because of the merger argument, there was no infringement.

The conclusion that the courts have drawn in cases where merger is successfully argued is that the only protection they will afford the author is against "virtually identical copying." In other words, to the extent that an author does find some special aspect of expression, that small aspect will be protected, but the indispensable expressive features, having been found to merge with the idea, can be copied freely.

THE SCENES A FAIRE DOCTRINE

There is a somewhat more general principle, referred to as the *scenes a faire* doctrine, which argues that standard ways of expressing common ideas should not be protected. An author using a well-known and commonly used plot, with the usual characters that go with it, should not be able to keep others from using that plot or the associated characters. Of course, there is the chicken-and-egg problem here: did the standard ways of expression become commonly accepted because of the popularity of an originally copyrighted work, or were those ways already standard at the time that copyright was established? Moreover, what does standard mean in this context? There are various degrees of acceptance, all of which are sometimes referred to as constituting a standard. We can identify one kind of standard as a *de facto* standard in the marketplace, such as the IBM Personal Computer has become, with all of its clones. No official body has proclaimed the IBM PC as a standard, but many people regard it as such.

An entirely different meaning for the word "standard" is the kind of standard established by official bodies, such as the American National Standards Institute, which issues standards only after a long and tortuous process. These standards, which cover, for example, almost everything consumers see in a typical hardware store, such as the threads on screws and light bulbs, may very well become enshrined in laws and regulations, and they are very different from *de facto* standards. The problem with the term "standard" is that most people use it loosely in everyday conversation, often just to mean that something is very popular. However, there are sometimes important legal consequences of such use, as in the application of the scenes a faire doctrine.

An interesting example of a scenes a faire argument was made by Microsoft in the *Apple Computer, Inc.* v. *Microsoft Corporation* case.[6] Microsoft prepared a videotape of user interfaces used in a number of products competing with the Macintosh and with the Microsoft Windows products at issue in the litigation. Relative to the perceived commonality of these user interfaces, Microsoft argued that the Apple user interface copyright should be deemed invalid because of a scenes a faire defense, even though most of the products using the so-called standard features came out after the Macintosh had established its popularity. Very likely those features were adopted because of the Macintosh popularity, thus making it the standard. The Microsoft case will be discussed further in Chapter 7.

Microsoft

Case: *Apple Computer, Inc.* v. *Microsoft Corporation and Hewlett-Packard Co.*,
          35 F.3d 1435 (1994)

Date: August 24, 1993

Summary: Apple had licensed Microsoft to use certain features of the operating systems on the Lisa and Macintosh computers. Microsoft had in turn licensed Hewlett-Packard to use its Windows application, which relied on Apple's system.

Subsequently, Apple charged Microsoft (and Hewlett-Packard) with copyright infringement, claiming that they had gone beyond the license provisions in marketing a user interface that was extremely similar to that of later versions of the Finder operating system.

Decision: The District Court found that the Microsoft user interface consisted almost entirely of elements that were either licensed or non-protectable. Therefore, there was no copyright infringement. The Appeals Court affirmed this decision.

NOTES

1. *Webster's New World Dictionary of the American Language*, 2nd College Edition, (New York: World Publishing Co, 1970), p. 723.

2. We saw in Chapter 5 that Rural Telephone Service Co. had used this device to establish that Feist Publications had copied data from Rural's white pages directory.

3. We shall discuss the concept of the clean room in Chapter 10, but it may be understood to be a method of producing software that is intended to establish convincingly that the work was done independently, and, therefore, without any copying, because there was no access to the original work.

4. *NEC, Inc.* v. *Intel, Inc.*, No. C-84-20799-WPG (N.D.Cal. Feb. 7, 1989), Section III.A.5.

5. Ibid., Section I.C

6. Apple also sued Hewlett-Packard for copyright infringement, and the two cases were joined.

7

Substantial Similarity

Now we come to the heart of the copyright infringement question, the issue of substantial similarity. At first glance it does not seem to be too difficult an issue. If the product alleged to be infringing looks pretty much like the original product and there was access, then there must have been copying.

But suppose it just looks a little like the other one? How similar do they have to be? How should similarity be measured? Does it make a difference if, except for a few similarities, the two products are very different? Suppose the two products are computer programs for which the source codes are clearly very different, but the screen presentations, that is, the user interfaces, are very similar? Somewhat similar? It gets complicated.

Let us take the simplest case. Consider two computer programs, written in the same language for the same computer, so comparison is possible, and in which a sizable number of lines of code in the two programs are identical. I claim then that it is unlikely that the two pieces of work were done independently. Why is that so?

First, it is possible that the code sequences in question were required in order to initiate a complex input or output action in the hardware. That kind of direct hardware/software interaction may indeed put enough constraints on the necessary code sequence that two people working independently would in fact come up with almost identical code. This is the situation that the merger argument envisages, and it is perfectly legitimate.

Let us assume, therefore, that there were no hardware or other constraints on the writing of the programs. There are then a great number of choices available to a programmer in choosing the actual instructions to be executed. For example, suppose we just want to put the value zero into one of the registers in the Arithmetic/Logic Unit (see Appendix A for further details). There are already several choices just to do that: (1) subtract whatever value is now in the register from itself; (2) shift whatever value is in the register enough places left or right so none of the original bits are still there, and only zeroes would have been shifted into the register; (3) load the constant value zero from a location in storage into the register; or (4) use an instruction available on most machines that has in the instruction itself the value zero to be loaded directly into the register. Just that simple transaction can be done in at least four different ways.

As another example, consider by analogy the several tasks that we might plan to do around the house on the coming weekend. It would be unusual if any of those tasks would require that one of the other tasks be done before it. Usually the tasks can be done in any order, such as mowing the lawn, repairing the bicycle tire, or vacuuming the rugs. In that situation, two people deciding independently what to do will probably not very likely come up with the same order in which to do those tasks. In a typical computer program, this situation arises very frequently; for example, a large number of rather small tasks must be carried out, but the order is not dictated by the problem to be solved. Two people working independently almost always will choose quite different orders in which to do those tasks.

Moreover, computer languages are not designed to have only the minimal number of ways to accomplish tasks. There are usually several ways to specify any computation or decision process. Take the question whether the value of a variable called "Year" is between 1980 and 1985. One way to write that test in a typical (but fictitious) high-level language is

```
If Year < 1980 or Year > 1985
    then print ("The year is outside the range.")
    else print ("The year is in the range 1980–85.")
```

Another way might be:

```
If Year ≥ 1980
    then if Year ≤ 1985
```

```
then print ("The year is in the range 1980-85.")
  else print ("The year is outside the range.")
else print ("The year is outside the range.")[1]
```

The second sequence of code shows a more complicated logical structure, but it produces exactly the same result as the first sequence. A programmer might very well think about the question to be asked in that more complicated way and write the code as in the second sequence.

Now consider that a typical program involves several hundred, or even thousands, of such code sequences, and it becomes clear why two people working independently will most often not come up with any sizable number of the same instruction sequences. Not only can they choose different code sequences, as in this example, but usually there are many choices as to the order in which to do them.

Does this mean that when we do find some identical lines in the two programs that there must have been copying? How many lines were identical? How many would it take to allow a conclusion of copyright infringement? In the SAS Institute case, the existence of 44 lines of identical code out of 186,000 total lines was enough, although there was other evidence of copyright infringement as well. On the other hand, the reluctance to rely too much on counting identical fragments is seen in the Whelan case: "There is no general requirement that most of each of two works be compared before a court can conclude that they are substantially similar. In the cases of literary works . . . the substantial similarity inquiry cannot be simply quantified. . . . Instead, the court must make a qualitative, not quantitative, judgment about the character of the work as a whole and the importance of the substantially similar portions of the work."

The fact is that it almost never comes down to comparing actual lines of code in programs written in the same language. Just as in charges of literary plagiarism, the usual case is that there is some similarity but not very much word-for-word copying. In a number of important cases, we see a view developing that at least some part of the design of a program and/or its user interface, as expressed in the resulting product, is protectable by copyright.

Thus, we have in the *Roth* v. *United Card* opinion: "It appears to us that in total concept and feel the cards of United are the same as the copyrighted cards of Roth . . . the characters depicted in the art work, the mood they portrayed, the combination of art work conveying a particular mood with a particular message, and the arrangement of the words . . . are substantially the same."

In the Broderbund case, the opinion states: "The ordinary observer could hardly avoid being struck by the eerie resemblance between the screens of the two programs. In general, the sequence of the screens and the choices presented, the layout of the screens, and the method of feedback to the user are all substantially similar." (We shall come back later to the reference to the ordinary observer.) Finally, in the SAS Institute opinion, we have: "to the extent that it represents copying of the organization and structural details of SAS, such copying pervades the entire S & H product." In Whelan: "We hold that . . . copyright protection of computer programs may extend beyond the programs' literal code to their structure, sequence, and organization."

That is not to say that this point of view has been universally popular in the computer industry. The Whelan decision has probably been attacked more often than any other decision affecting the industry, except perhaps the decision to issue patents for software-related inventions. To some extent, this is understandable. Programmers look at such a decision and wonder how they can tell when they might be accused of copying someone else's "total concept and feel." They would like a world in which they can use anyone's ideas as long as they do not copy their expression. To most programmers, however, "expression" means "code," and everything else is "idea." As indicated above, however, many choices that come in through the design process are being recognized as part of the expression of the idea, and it is becoming clear that programmers are expected to design their own solutions to their problems, as well as write their own code.

The same resistance to constraints by programmers appears in the reaction to the protection of user-interface elements, as in the *Lotus* v. *Paperback* decision, which shall be considered in detail in Chapter 8. Many programmers believe that as long as they write their own code, they should be entitled to use whatever they can observe or learn from someone else's work. The usual argument is that this is what the public wants. To be sure, there is an argument that the public would prefer not to have to retrain their employees or relearn a new system or interface in order to take advantage of some new features in a competing product. In balancing that public interest against the benefits of copyright protection, however, the courts have leaned in the direction of protection, based on the original intent of the Copyright Law; that is, to encourage innovation in the public interest. It is not asking too much of a programmer, after seeing someone else's good idea, to develop that idea in program form using his or her own talents. In most cases where a conflict in this arena has reached litigation, it has not been an accident.

As Clapes and associates put it: "In the real world, . . . software copyright infringement claims do not arise merely because two programs serve a single, identifiable purpose or set of purposes. . . . First, in every case there has been not only access but extensive access to the copyrighted original. Second, the alleged infringer has explicitly traded on user-recognizable similarities . . . the challenged similarity between the two programs was not fortuitous."[2]

If some observer is going to judge similarity, how expert must that person be? If a copyright case involves an historical novel, should the person who makes the comparison be a historian trained in the period of history under consideration? If the case involves computer programs, should the person be an expert programmer? One could make the argument that because the products are usually competing for a consumer's attention in some market, the observer should be a typical person in that market, to see if the alleged similarities are apparent to such a person. If not, there is not enough similarity to worry about, according to that line of reasoning.

Because the use of substantial similarity is really to determine whether copying of protected material has occurred, the issue is not just the economic issue that the potential buyer of the products may not be able to differentiate between them. Even when the final product has been changed enough so the differences are clear, there may still be the question of damages, as we indicated earlier, for the period of time in which there was confusion and reduction of market share, as well as savings from the earlier time-to-market for the copied product, because of the shorter development period.

A reasonable two-part process has been articulated, although it has evolved somewhat over the years. In *Arnstein* v. *Porter* we find: "The trier of fact must determine whether the similarities are sufficient to prove copying. . . . If copying is established, then only does there arise the second issue, that of illicit copying (unlawful appropriation)."[3]

Arnstein

Case: *Arnstein* v. *Porter*,
           154 F.2d 464 (2d Cir. 1946)

Date: February 11, 1946

Summary: Ira Arnstein sued Cole Porter for copyright infringement on
           such well-known songs as "Begin the Beguine," "My Heart
           Belongs to Daddy," "Night and Day," "Don't Fence Me In,"

and "You'd Be So Nice to Come Home To." Porter denied in his deposition that he had ever seen or heard any of Arnstein's compositions. The issues included whether the case should go to trial or be settled by summary judgement based on the depositions, and the role of experts in determining substantial similarity in musical compositions.

Decision: The court decided that summary judgement was not justified, and that the case should go to trial.

This is a little confusing, and in the Krofft case this ruling was clarified. Using the example of an inexpensive nude statue, the court determined that the first stage, corresponding roughly to the Arnstein first stage, was to test for similarity of ideas. "A statue of a horse or a painting of a nude would not embody [the *idea* of a plaster recreation of a nude human figure], and therefore could not infringe."

The court referred to this as the "extrinsic test," because "it depends . . . on specific criteria which can be listed and analyzed." If it is determined that there was indeed similarity of the ideas involved, a second step must be taken to determine whether there was substantial similarity of the expression of the ideas. This is called the "intrinsic test," because "it does not depend on the type of external criteria and analysis which marks the extrinsic test."

Sid & Marty Krofft

Case: *Sid & Marty Krofft Television Prod, Inc.* v. *McDonald's Corp.*,
562 F.2d 1157 (9th Cir. 1977)

Date: October 12, 1977

Summary: Krofft had created a television show, H. R. Pufnstuf, which was very successful, and which had led to separate licenses for other products based on the show. They had had discussions with an advertising agency, Needham, Harper & Steers, about cooperating on an ad campaign for McDonald's. Later Krofft was told the campaign was cancelled, but in fact it proceeded without them. Various commercials and licenses were generated by McDonald's based on the Krofft characters, and Krofft sued for copyright infringement. In a jury trial, Krofft prevailed, but appealed the amount of damages. The defendant appealed several legal issues. The issues included the process by which substantial similarity was determined. The two-step test developed here, of finding similarity first of the idea(s) and then of the expression of the idea(s), has become a standard for later trials. This opinion also elaborated the basis for determining similarity for each step, and the roles of expert witnesses and the "trier of fact" (that is, the jury, if there is one, or the trial judge) in the process.

Decision: The Appeals Court affirmed the judgement of the District Court with respect to infringement, but remanded the case back to the lower court for reconsideration of the damages.

If the two products being compared do not share even one or more common ideas, there could not have been copying, so the process might as well end with a conclusion of no copying. If there are common ideas, there might have been copying, so look for similarities in the expression. There is still the question in each of these steps as to who should be making the decisions — ordinary observers, as in a jury, or experts.

Most courts have recognized the appropriateness of this "two-step rule," but some have decided not to use it as articulated here. More precisely, in addition to spelling out the two steps, the court in the Krofft case specified that in the first step, just as in the Arnstein opinion, it was appropriate to elicit expert testimony specific to the content of the technical field involved. This takes into account the kind of analysis that is needed to understand the issues and the components of the works in question.

However, both the Arnstein and Krofft opinions specified that a jury was uniquely qualified to determine whether the expression was substantially similar, once the ideas have been found to be similar. As the Arnstein court put it: "the test is the response of the ordinary lay [person]; . . . on that issue, 'dissection' and expert testimony are irrelevant."[4]

The reason that the Whelan court decided not to honor those precedents was that in that court's opinion, the issues involved with computer programs were so complex that expert testimony was needed even at the second stage. Both the District Court and the Appeals Court explicitly decided to use an integrated test involving both lay and expert testimony. In Broderbund, the court recognized the process adopted in Whelan, even referring to it as a possible "wave of the future," but then that court decided to conform to the Krofft rule, and the bifurcated test, using experts for the extrinsic test and the "ordinary observer" for the intrinsic test. The Broderbund court then wrote: "The ordinary observer could hardly avoid being struck by the eerie resemblance between the screens of the two programs."

One of the main controversies in the Microsoft case arises from the question of dissection. Although Apple contended all along that it was concerned with the overall similarity of appearance between the Windows screen presentation and that of the Lisa and Macintosh user interfaces,[5] Microsoft persuaded the court to require Apple to list all of the specific similarities it thought appeared in the two screen presentations. Then the court proceeded to consider each of the items on the list separately, applying the dissection analysis to determine substantial similarity. Apple would have preferred the kind of conclusion that appeared in the opinion of the Broderbund court: "Mere lists of similarities cannot adequately convey the impression of overall similarity between 'Print Shop' and 'Printmaster.' No ordinary observer could reasonably conclude that the expression of the ideas underlying these two programs were not substantially similar. . . . The 'total concept and feel' of these programs . . . is virtually identical. The application of the intrinsic test in the present case compels the finding that their expression is substantially similar."

The complexity of the Microsoft litigation was compounded by the existence of a license that Apple had granted to Microsoft to settle a previous allegation of copyright infringement with respect to the Lisa and Macintosh interfaces. Once the court began to dissect the interface components, it ruled that some of those components had been licensed by the earlier agreement. In addition, there were the scenes a faire arguments that we have already seen; products that had appeared on the market long after the infringement charges were made apparently were considered as contributing to the standard nature of some of the components.

The reasoning of the Microsoft court regarding dissection was supported in the Altai case. The Appeals Court in the Second Circuit outlined the appropriate sequence of steps as follows:

In ascertaining substantial similarity under this approach, a court would first break down the allegedly infringed program into its constituent structural parts. Then, by examining each of these parts for such things as incorporated ideas, expression that is necessarily incidental to those ideas, and elements that are taken from the public domain, a court would then be able to sift out all non-protectable material. Left with a kernel, or possibly kernels, of creative expression after following this process of elimination, the court's last step would be to compare this material with the structure of an allegedly infringing program. The result of this comparison will determine whether the protectable elements of the programs at issue are substantially similar so as to warrant a finding of infringement.[6]

The question of dissection is not settled, however. A recent Appeals Court decision, in *Gates Rubber Co.* v. *Bando American, Inc.*, partly agrees with the Altai opinion, in approving the "abstraction-filtration-comparison" (AFC) test, but significantly differs from the Altai opinion in providing for an overall comparison of the works in question before applying that test. In a clear and well-written attempt to reconcile the diverse rulings in different circuits that preceded this opinion, the 10th Circuit Appeal Court states (footnote 7, citations omitted):

In examining the similarities between two programs under the indirect method of proving copying [which requires showing access and substantial similarities] it is ordinarily important to compare the whole works. . . . We acknowledge that unprotectable elements of a program, even if copied verbatim, cannot serve as the basis for ultimate liability for copyright infringement. However, the copying of even unprotected elements can have a probative value in determining whether the defendant copied the plaintiff's work. Where a court first extracts all unprotected elements of a work, and only compares protected elements, it deprives itself of the use of probative, and potentially essential, information on the factual issue of copying. That is because, even if a court finds protectable elements of a program to be similar, it must still determine whether those elements were copied from the plaintiff's work, whether the duplication can be attributed to other factors, or whether its reproduction was pure chance. The fact that non-protectable elements of the original program were also copied, although it cannot be the basis for liability, can be probative of whether protected elements were copied. That is because, in certain conditions, it may be more likely that protected elements were copied if there is evidence of copying among the unprotected elements of the program.

Because the Gates Rubber Co. case was heard in a different region from the Altai case, it may very well take a Supreme Court decision on the dissection issue to resolve it definitively.

Gates Rubber

Case: *Gates Rubber Co.* v. *Bando American, Inc.*,
             9 F.3rd 829 (10th Cir., 1993)

Date: October 19, 1993

Original decision: June 24, 1992

Summary: Gates Rubber created a program, called Design Flex 4.0, which is used by their marketing people to help design systems which could use their replacement belts. Soon after leaving Gates, several former employees began demonstrating Chauffeur, a competing and similar program, which Gates charged was based on trade secrets taken by the former employees, and which violated their copyright on Design Flex 4.0.

Decision: Summary judgment was granted, and the defendants were ordered to cease and desist use of the Chauffeur program. The Appeals Court upheld the trade secrets part of the earlier decision, but remanded the case to the District Court for further clarification and consideration of a number of copyright issues.

In the same opinion, the Gates Rubber Appeals Court suggests that the comparison of the works as a whole come first: "It will often be helpful to make an initial determination of whether the defendant copied portions of the plaintiff's program before determining whether the copying involved protectable elements under the copyright law," but they do recommend applying this procedure on a case-by-case basis.

It seems to me that the recommended procedure of comparing the works as a whole and then applying the AFC test is unnecessarily complicated. It would seem that an alternative procedure, the ACF test, would take care of much of the difficulty and confusion we are seeing here. This procedure would identify the levels of abstraction inherent in the original program; the Gates Rubber Appeals Court opinion makes some very helpful suggestions along these lines. Then the comparison for similarities could be made (including the works as a whole). This would allow a reasonable determination of copying. Then the filtration could be applied, to determine whether those elements that have been determined to have been copied were, in fact, protected. (Some protectable elements may no longer be protected, as in the Microsoft case, where the license may have allowed the use of some otherwise protectable elements.)

Since the Gates Rubber Co. case was heard in a different circuit from the Altai case, it may very well take a Supreme Court decision on the dissection issue to resolve it definitively. In fact, on December 19, 1994, Apple Computer, Inc. filed a "Petition for Writ of Certiorari to the United States Court of Appeals for the Ninth Circuit," which is a request to the United States Supreme Court to review the decision of the Appeals Court in the *Apple Computer, Inc.* v. *Microsoft Corporation et al.* case. One of the primary questions presented to the Supreme Court in that petition is: "Is the standard of protection for a computer graphical user interface subject to diminution by judicial 'dissection' of the work and 'filtration' of those 'elements' the court deems licensed or unprotectible [*sic*], without regard to the defendant's copying of the creative aspects of the work as a whole?"

Returning to the Altai case, the court retained an expert, Prof. Randall Davis of the Massachusetts Institute of Technology, to advise it on technical matters. Prof. Davis's analysis led the court to severely criticize and apparently abandon the Whelan point of view, although it is not at all clear that after the critical remarks were made the subsequent opinion made any use of the distinctions that were introduced by Prof. Davis. According to the court:

Central to Dr. Davis's criticism of the Whelan "structure, sequence, and organization" formulation is the fact that there is no necessary relationship between the sequence of operations in a program, which are part of behavior, and the order or sequence in which those operations are set forth in the text of the program — the source code and object code. As Dr. Davis pointed out, "the order in which sub-routines appear in the program text is utterly irrelevant," and the two views of a computer program, as text and as behavior, are "quite distinct."

Each view — textual and behavioral — has its own structure, sequence, and organization. In the standard jargon of programmers, there is static structure, which refers to the program-as-text view, and dynamic structure, which refers to the program-as-behavior view. The static structure and dynamic structure of a program can be quite different; indeed from dealing with behavior of a program, i.e., operating it, one can tell virtually nothing about its text. Thus, according to Dr. Davis, "it makes no technical sense to talk simply about the 'structure' of a program, because the term is ambiguous and the distinction [between dynamic structure and static structure] matters."

Whelan, therefore, is fundamentally flawed, according to Dr. Davis, by failing to distinguish between the static and dynamic views of a program.[7, 8]

The problem is that the court then went on to analyze the case at hand without ever referring to the distinction that had been made. The Davis distinction may indeed be useful, but the way to take advantage of it would be to understand that either of the kinds of structure (static or dynamic) could actually be substantially similar, independently, and would then serve as an indication of possible copying.

More specifically, if we go back once more to the many choices any software designer must make, including which sub-routines to employ in the first place, and then on to which parameters to use to communicate between sub-routines, we see that there are always behavioral aspects in those choices. These behavioral aspects lead to the selection of which component functionalities to package into sub-routines, how complex to make each of them, whether one large sub-routine should in fact be broken into several smaller ones, and in which sequence they might call each other. Textual aspects, such as in the choices of actual sequences of statements to write, and which macros to define and package, are also affected (see Appendix A for details on these topics). Sometimes it might be helpful to sort these out so as to better understand where copying might have occurred and where specific changes might have been made to avoid the appearance of copying. At other times it might not prove useful, as it apparently did not in the Altai case.

The alleged flaw in the Whelan decision was to not make the Davis distinction explicit. In Whelan, the court decided to use the terms "structure," "sequence," and "organization" as essentially equivalent. They missed the opportunity to differentiate between the static representation of a program as text and the dynamic representation as behavior. Structure and organization would normally be considered to refer to the static form, while sequence would normally have dynamic connotations. While I do not believe that considering these different aspects together invalidates the Whelan decision, it might be helpful for future courts to better clarify the Davis distinction and then to base decisions more explicitly on the kinds of similarities that would then be exposed.

The Altai opinion introduced another disturbing kind of analysis, based on the advice of Prof. Davis:

Taking an overall view of "similarity," Dr. Davis attempted to quantify the relative importance of the various factors of similarity on which [Computer Associates] relied. He evaluated them as follows:

Code	1,000
Parameter Lists	100
Macros	100
List of Services	1
Organization Chart	Nil

As applied to [the program involved], the factor which is by far the most important — code, rated at 1,000 — presents no similarity at all, because the code was rewritten.

In my opinion as a computer scientist, it is ridiculous to try to assign such weights in any particular case, let alone in general. It would be most difficult to find agreement in the software community that such weights were appropriate at all, and impossible to find agreement on what the values should be.

NOTES

1. In this example, ≤ means less than or equal to, and ≥ means greater than or equal to.
2. Clapes, A., Lynch, P., and Steinberg, R., "Silicon Epics and Binary Bards: Determining the Proper Scope of Copyright Protection for Computer Programs," *UCLA Law Review* 34(5 & 6) (1987): 1493–1594.
3. The trier of fact is the jury, if there is one, or the trial judge if it is not a jury trial.
4. Dissection is the separation of the works in question into comparable components, which presumably needs an expert's opinion.
5. The Macintosh is a very popular personal computer produced by Apple Computer, Inc. The Lisa was an earlier Apple product which shared many of the Macintosh's characteristics.
6. The Appeals Court found that the District Court had erred in dissecting the infringing program instead of the infringed program. The higher court decided that the result was the same, however, in this case.
7. This is not entirely correct, technically, because some translators infer specific relationships among sub-routines from their order, and moving some sub-routine definitions around in the text might in some cases generate error conditions.
8. In reviewing a draft of this manuscript, a computer scientist who was active in the computing field for over 40 years commented: "I have been in computing for quite a while, but have rarely if ever heard about 'textual' and 'behavioral' structure, or 'static' structure or 'dynamic' structure. I think most people will be confused by this." That is my own opinion based on my experience, also.

8

Look and Feel

It is not surprising that the result of the *Lotus Development Corp.* v. *Paperback Software International, Inc.* case raised a great controversy in the trade press in 1991. The issue in the Lotus case, according to the press, was "look and feel," although the parties did not use the term, and the court explicitly disclaimed it: "Despite its widespread use in public discourse on the copyrightability of nonliteral elements of computer programs, I have not found the 'look and feel' concept, standing alone, to be significantly helpful in distinguishing between nonliteral elements of a computer program that are copyrightable and those that are not."

While the issue in this case was the creative expression in the user interface of the Lotus product called "1-2-3," the real look and feel issues of the user interface surfaced in the Microsoft case discussed in Chapter 7.

Lotus

Case: *Lotus Development Corp.* v. *Paperback Software Int'l*, 740 F.Supp 37 (D. Mass. 1990)

Date: June 28, 1990

Summary: Lotus Development had marketed a very successful spread-sheet program, named 1-2-3. Paperback had originally planned to market their VP-Planner product with different capabilities and a different "menu tree," which guides the user through the problem-solving decision process. With the market success of 1-2-3, Paperback modified its product to mimic almost completely the menu tree of 1-2-3, arguing that it was necessary to compete in the marketplace. The primary issue to be decided was the scope of the copyright protection of the 1-2-3 program; that is, whether it included the "non-literal" part of the expression, the menu tree.

Decision: The menu tree is protectable expression, and Paperback Software had indeed infringed the Lotus copyright.

THE SPREADSHEET

The Lotus 1-2-3 product is a spreadsheet, which displays a grid of cells that can contain either numeric values or strings of characters.[1] Some of the character strings represent "labels," to be interpreted as names or headings for rows or columns of reports, the typical application of 1-2-3. Other character strings consist of abbreviations for sequences of command words (or their first letters), which direct 1-2-3 to carry out specific functions, or to combine other values in the grid to generate new values to be placed in cells in the grid.

As one example of the use of this very general tool, one can visualize a spreadsheet for an income tax form, with labels identifying the rows of the form, and dollar amounts in certain columns representing the tax computation values. The benefit of using a computerized spreadsheet comes in the ability to specify that the value in a certain grid cell is to be computed from certain others according to a specified formula. (The typical tax form instructs us to do the same kind of computations for each line, usually in words in small print.) In the spreadsheet, if any of the values used in the computation ever changes, the formula is automatically invoked again to recompute all affected values. This eliminates much erasing and rewriting, and, of course, many errors.

We could expect to create, or buy, such an income tax spreadsheet program, and during the tax season to put dollar amounts into various cells in the grid when these amounts become available, usually from employers or banks, during the month of January. Each time an amount is entered, such as the interest earned in a bank account, every computed value that depends on that interest will be recomputed, bringing the displayed form a little closer to the final tax return. One additional advantage of using such a program is the ability to explore the consequences of varying some amount; that is, doing a "what-if" type of analysis. For example, one could ask about the effect on the bottom line of an increase in the state income tax rate or a decrease in the bank's interest rate.

During the development of a spreadsheet program, the user needs to communicate with the 1-2-3 software itself, to specify whether an amount of money is to be represented in dollars or in English pounds, for example, or whether a column of numbers is to be lined up on the decimal point, or right-justified. Because it is also possible to save partial spreadsheets in files for later recall and use, it is also necessary to name these files and specify their formats. In addition, when a report is to be printed, several options are available as to how to print it, such as with the grid lines printed or suppressed, and so on. As a result of these options and the need to communicate with 1-2-3 to specify which option to choose at any given time, the designers of 1-2-3 provided a menu of choices, and a method of selection from the menu in order to specify a choice.

The selection method actually guides the user of the spreadsheet through a sequence of menus. Each selection from a menu determines the next part of the menu tree, that is, the next menu, to be offered to the user for selection. Figure 8.1 shows a typical workstation screen containing a partially completed 1-2-3 spreadsheet, and Figure 8.2 shows the part of the full 1-2-3 menu tree that was used in generating Figure 8.1.

Note that the top line on the spreadsheet shown in Figure 8.1 shows the text just entered by the user, or the currently available choices, corresponding to a particular level of choice in the menu tree. Whenever choices are displayed on the top line, the current choice that can be selected by merely pushing a particular button, is highlighted.

The second line on the spreadsheet provides, in some cases, the set of choices that will be made available if the current choice on the top line is indeed selected. In other cases, a short explanation of the effect of choosing the currently available item on the top line is presented.

The rest of the screen contains the grid itself, or at least a portion of it, like looking through a magnifying glass at a portion of a printed page. In 1-2-3, as in most spreadsheets, the rows and columns are identified by means of letters or numbers, so one might refer to a particular cell in the grid as Q31, meaning row Q, column 31, although one can also refer to cells in other ways.

Users of spreadsheets often find themselves repeating the same sequence of menu commands many times, such as the commands needed to set up a particular report and print it in a certain format. In 1-2-3, as in many spreadsheet products, it is possible to record once and for all the

FIGURE 8.1
An Example of Lotus 1-2-3 Spreadsheet

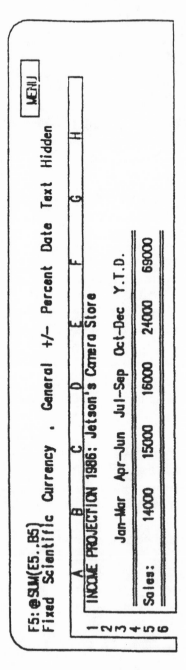

FIGURE 8.2
Part of the Lotus 1-2-3 Menu Tree

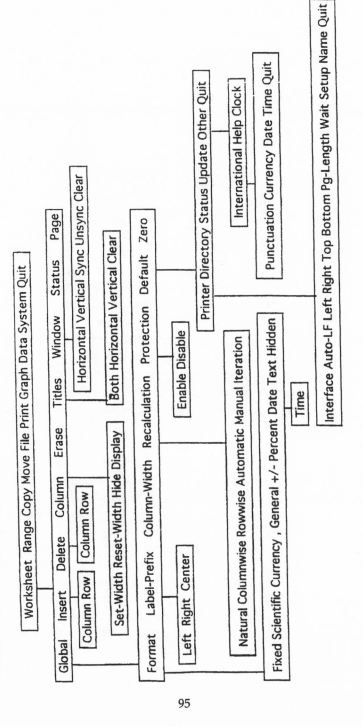

sequence needed to carry out a particular complicated function of this kind, name it for later recall, and store it away. This package of commands is called a "macro," similar to the macros discussed in Appendix A, and it is a valuable labor saver. Moreover, macros make it possible to package complete spreadsheet programs, such as an entire income tax package, and market them. The end user is merely instructed to enter from the keyboard a familiar-sounding label, which turns out to be the name of a macro, and it executes a completely pre-packaged set of commands that prompts the user for input, calculates the final results, and prints out the completed tax form.

The History of the Lotus 1-2-3 Litigation

Lotus's 1-2-3 was not the first spreadsheet product on the market, but its predecessor, Visicalc, had some limitations that made its entry into the market somewhat more difficult than its designers had hoped. When 1-2-3 became available, a carefully orchestrated advertising campaign came with it, and 1-2-3 caught on very quickly. In many ways, it was a long-sought-after solution to an entire class of problems, those whose solutions could be set up as a collection of interdependent computations using a relatively small set of input values, such as the income tax form.

The 1-2-3 product became an industry leader almost overnight. In the years since the introduction of 1-2-3 in the early 1980s, several competitors have also marketed spreadsheet programs, some quite successfully.[2] In most of these competitive spreadsheet programs, the menu tree of commands available to the user at any time is quite different from that of 1-2-3, although all use the grid format for the spreadsheet. It is common in the industry — and not considered proprietary — to describe the grid as "an inverted L." The intended visual image is that of the letters down the side and the numbers across the top, which label the rows and columns. A few spreadsheet products provide a special command that replaces the standard menu tree for that product with that of 1-2-3, so people trained on 1-2-3 can continue using its familiar terms and commands even if they change products or organizations. Two companies, however, did not attempt to market their own menu tree, but adopted that of 1-2-3 entirely, with a few small additions of their own, and that led to the litigation that caught the industry's attention.

James Stephenson, the author of VP-Planner, a product of one of the two companies that adopted the 1-2-3 menu tree entirely, had already been developing a product based on the ideas of Visicalc when he saw a demonstration of 1-2-3 in early 1983. As his testimony indicates, in 1984 he realized that 1-2-3 was going to be very successful, and he and his colleagues came to the conclusion that the only way for them to compete was to be completely compatible with 1-2-3. One of the issues in the trial was the proper definition of "compatible" in this context.

One important reason for compatibility in the software industry is to be able to woo customers away from their current software. Every user of an application program like 1-2-3 builds a library of spreadsheet programs such as the income tax package we have described. A company that bases much of its data storage and report generation on a spreadsheet package like 1-2-3 will create such a library, not only of spreadsheet programs but of data files. Thus, there is a strong barrier to changing from a package in current use to a different spreadsheet package, even a new package with additional desirable features and services. The change is made easier if the new package is compatible with the old one. Spreadsheet programs that run successfully on the current package will continue to run successfully on the new one. Another positive aspect of compatibility is that employees who have learned to use the current package will not have to be retrained on another, unfamiliar system.

Some of the questions raised in the Lotus case were: (1) Are there degrees of compatibility? (2) How compatible does a new product have to be in order to compete successfully with an established product? At one extreme, a new product can be designed to be totally incompatible with other products, but with so many wonderful new features and improved performance that it can compete just because of those features. At the other end, one can decide that every detail of every existing program, including pre-packaged macros and existing historical data, must run with the new product with absolutely no changes needed at all.[3]

Between these two extremes lie several possibilities, however. Some vendors have created their own spreadsheet programs with different menu trees and have provided translation software to help convert existing programs and data into a form which can be processed by their new products. Such translations need to be done only once, because the translation software reads the existing spreadsheet programs and generates new spreadsheet programs, expressed in the command structure of the new product. The historical data is read according to the formatting and data structure of the old product, and it is recreated in the format and structure of the new product. The results of these translations of the spreadsheet programs and data are then stored away, and are available from then on to be run with the new product. Further translation is not needed. Occasionally, a new spreadsheet program might be acquired from another organization that was generated using the previous spreadsheet software, and then a one-time translation would be applied to that program.

It turns out that, with some effort, one can create examples of sophisticated macros that are not easily translated in their entirety into another menu tree or may not be translatable at all. To this extent, one can claim that the new product is not completely compatible, and then a business decision must be made as to how to treat this degree of incompatibility in selling the product. One important example, which was demonstrated at the trial, is the Excel spreadsheet software of Microsoft, Inc., a quite successful competitor to 1-2-3. The translator provided with the Excel spreadsheet software does a very good job translating 1-2-3 spreadsheet programs, data, and macros into Excel spreadsheet programs, data, and macros, except for a few macros that use some subtle features of the 1-2-3 command menu. For those exceptional cases, the Excel translator generates a warning in boldface type, calling attention to these exceptions, and recommending their translation by hand, after additional scrutiny by an expert. Once that further translation is accomplished the job need not be done again.

There are other possible ways of handling the compatibility problem, such as interpreting Lotus 1-2-3 commands and macros as they occur during execution. This could take care of most, if not all, of even the exceptional cases, but there might be a great deal of overhead in terms of execution time, and most vendors would not want to incur that overhead. The designers of Excel apparently decided not to do interpretation each time a 1-2-3 spreadsheet program was to be run. Instead, they relied on the warning generated whenever the one-time translation could not be accomplished without additional human analysis.

Paperback Software[4] made the decision, as reported in its testimony, that the company needed full compatibility, even as far as executing all possible macros, and that this could only be accomplished by adopting the exact command menu tree of 1-2-3. Paperback added some additional features and claimed that, by adding the selection terms for the new features to the end of each relevant menu line on the screen, the relative positions of the command choices would remain the same, keeping old 1-2-3 macros executable. Without going into the detail, it was shown at the trial that adding such additional features ruled out complete macro compatibility in any case, so even that part of the argument was weakened.

Paperback also argued that it was necessary for its product to have "two-way macro compatibility." This meant that in addition to having 1-2-3 macros execute correctly on their product, VP-Planner, macros generated by the use of VP-Planner must be executable exactly by 1-2-3, in case someone needed to exchange information with a friend that he or she had just written in VP-Planner. Of course, if the new macro used any of the additional features Paperback had added to the menu tree, 1-2-3 would not have recognized these commands. Giving such a macro to a friend who used 1-2-3 would have been impossible, but that was the argument that was used.

There were other issues in the Paperback Software defense, such as arguing that because spreadsheet software was "useful," it should not be copyrightable, and that certain terms, such as "print," were so functional and uniquely expressive for the print function they should not be protected. Therefore, Paperback argued, the entire menu and, in fact, the entire interface should not be copyrightable.

Judge Robert Keeton's opinion explained on each count why such arguments were not persuasive. In short, he determined that the command menu tree was different from the idea of the spreadsheet itself, that a particular menu structure was different from the idea of a menu structure, that while some aspects of a spreadsheet were utilitarian, other aspects were not, and that the menu tree, in particular, was an example of creative expression, because there were many different ways to create menu trees, as had actually been done in a number of competitive products:

This particular expression of a menu structure is not essential to the electronic spreadsheet idea, nor does it merge with the somewhat less abstract idea of a menu structure for an electronic spreadsheet. The idea of a menu structure . . . could be expressed in a great many if not literally unlimited number of ways.

The fact that some of these specific command terms are quite obvious or merge with the idea of such a particular command term does not preclude copyrightability for the command structure taken as a whole. If particular characteristics not distinctive individually have been brought together in a way that makes the "whole" a distinctive expression of an idea — one of many possible ways of expressing it — then the "whole" may be copyrightable.

. . .

I conclude that a menu command structure is capable of being expressed in many if not an unlimited number of ways, and that the command structure of 1-2-3 is an original and nonobvious way of expressing a command structure.

Consequences of the *Lotus* v. *Paperback* Case

There were two immediate consequences of the Lotus victory in the Paperback case. Within days, Lotus filed suit against two other spreadsheet vendors, Borland and The Santa Cruz Operation (SCO). In both cases, the spreadsheet products were based on different menu structures; however, one of the first selections a user could make was to replace the so-called "native" menu structure with that of 1-2-3. From that point on, the spreadsheet software would behave in every respect like 1-2-3, including data formats and macros.

Having won the right to copyright its menu structure, and the representation of that structure on the screen, Lotus contended that these other vendors did not have the right to offer it within their products as a complete alternative to their own menu structure. The issue now was not copyrightability, although the Borland defense raised that argument again, but whether the way these other vendors included the 1-2-3 menu structures constituted infringement. The case against SCO was settled quite quickly in Lotus's favor; in a subsequent decision, Judge Keeton ruled that Borland did in fact infringe the Lotus 1-2-3 copyright.

Borland

Case: *Lotus Development Corp.* v. *Borland International, Inc.*, 831 F.Supp. 223 (D. Mass. 1993)

Date: July 31, 1992

Summary: Lotus charged that Borland violated its copyright on the 1-2-3 spreadsheet by providing direct access to the 1-2-3 menu tree and other features. Borland had its own "native" menu tree in Quattro Pro, but provided a single command to convert the user interface to that of 1-2-3, with a few additions. Lotus asked that Borland be constrained from providing that easy conversion to the 1-2-3 interface.

Decision: The court decided that Borland had indeed violated the Lotus copyright and enjoined Borland from providing the direct access to the 1-2-3 user interface.

The other effect of the Lotus opinion has been to increase the outcry against protecting user interfaces at all. During the *Lotus* v. *Paperback* trial, one expert witness for Paperback Software stated: "If aspects of screen displays that are governed by functionality (such as a command language like the 1-2-3 command structure) are held to be within the scope of copyright protection, then progress in application and systems computer programs could be dramatically slowed in the United States."[5]

Another expert witness for Paperback Software introduced an opinion based on a survey of leading user interface designers at a conference, stating that these designers opposed strong copyright protection for elements of a user interface because such protection would be harmful to the industry. Groups of people in the Boston area have picketed outside the Lotus headquarters building to protest its copyright litigation. Why do these people, who are very involved in and committed to the industry, believe that all of this will be so harmful? Why do others believe with equal fervor that copyright protection is beneficial for the industry?

SOME HISTORY

The roots of this controversy appear to go back to the early days of modern computing, in the 1940s and 1950s. The programmable computer was a new invention, and at that time no one had written very much software. Every new algorithm or program was exciting. A well-written, elegant sorting routine, an efficient print program, or a simple loader that would fit on a single punched card was freely given away and sometimes even publicly recognized at conferences. The SHARE organization, for example, was formed by users of large IBM computers precisely for the purpose of exchanging software freely, so programmers would not have to reinvent solutions to common problems. Recognition and honor were based on the elegance of problem solutions presented in the form of programs and on how widely their use spread throughout the country.

In those early days, no one sold or even considered selling software. It was clear that everyone benefitted from the free exchange of programs. It was only when more and more complex software began to be developed that the institutions producing this software started to try to recover some of the costs involved. It soon became clear that the tide toward treating software as a commercial product could not be stopped. With the advent of high-level languages, the proliferation of time-sharing applications, the introduction of the computer into the office, and the subsequent influence on every other aspect of daily life, there was an explosion in the need for and the availability of both system programs and application programs.

A key event in this evolution was the decision by IBM in 1969 to "unbundle" its software. When computers were first offered commercially, there was essentially no software industry. Because the hardware was nonfunctional without software, IBM and other systems suppliers provided rudimentary operating systems to provide the basic functions, but the users generally wrote the application software. In addition to the informal distribution described above and the activities of SHARE, IBM and other system suppliers served as major distributors of software and, in some cases, even as maintainers of the software they distributed. This distribution system persisted even when operating systems became more and more complex. Because software was the product that helped sell the hardware, the systems suppliers were not particularly concerned that there was no revenue tied to the software as such.

In the latter half of the 1960s, the costs of writing, maintaining, and distributing the software became so large that they could no longer be ignored. During that same period, the first software houses were established, and they found that they could compete even with the free software by offering more attractive products. The availability of the free software inhibited their business, however. Antitrust challenges were anticipated by the system suppliers, and they voluntarily acted, led by IBM, to separate the selling of software and hardware. This unbundling led to a rapid growth in the number of software houses, and the software industry was established.

Once the software industry was born, of course, it became necessary for authors to protect their intellectual property. If others could copy their products as soon as they came to market, why invest large amounts of time and money to create software? In fact, software is one of the easiest kinds of intellectual property to copy, because the computer is available to do the work. There was a period of great confusion during the 1970s, because the Copyright Office and the U.S. Patent & Trademark Office changed their minds on a number of occasions on whether to issue copyrights and/or patents. Finally, as we have seen, Congress adopted the Copyright Act of 1976, set up the National Commission on New Technological Uses of Copyrighted Works, and amended the Copyright Act in 1980 based on the commission's recommendations, to explicitly provide copyright protection for software. We have already discussed the situation with software patents in Chapter 3.

THE CURRENT DEBATE

It is against this background that the current controversy over the protection of user interfaces should be viewed. Some leaders of the opposition to such protection, those in favor of the free use of popular interface components in particular, are well-known university faculty, who no doubt remember the days of free exchange and the benefits they and others derived from that exchange. They would probably argue that a return to that kind of mutual support and encouragement would be beneficial to the industry. But just as the new software industry in the 1970s and 1980s needed protection for its intellectual property, developers of the most recently recognized aspects of software, the user interfaces, also need protection for their intellectual products.

In part, the argument for less protection is the fear that the rights granted under copyright and patent protection give inventors too much power to withhold their work from others. While experience with software patents is too recent to be able to judge that aspect at this time, the history of software copyrights does not support this fear. It is true that there is litigation, such as in the Lotus case, to retain copyright protection, but that is different from a refusal to license others to use the protected products. I have not observed a trend in the industry toward refusal to license, although the license often comes laden with severe restrictions, such as we discuss in the *Atari Games Corp.* v. *Nintendo of America, Inc.* and *Sega Enterprises Ltd.* v. *Accolade, Inc.* cases in Chapter 9.

For those who do fear excessive power in intellectual property protection, the remedy is to create something better. An instructive example of this interplay is the history of a now obscure computer language, COMIT. The author of COMIT refused to let anyone change the language he had designed, a language very well suited for the manipulation of strings of characters. A number of people had suggested improvements in the COMIT language, and it might have become very popular if he had listened to these suggestions and let the language evolve to take advantage of the insights of his friends. Instead, he held on very tightly to the original form of the language, as he had specified it.

The result of the inflexible attitude taken with COMIT was that a small group of researchers at AT&T's Bell Laboratories designed a similar but different language, called SNOBOL, which borrowed many ideas from COMIT but had its own syntax, and which incorporated the many additional ideas that had been suggested for COMIT. SNOBOL became very popular, and still has many devoted followers, while hardly anyone in the industry has heard of COMIT.

"Copyright Suits Could Slow Innovation" was the headline of an article in the trade press after the Lotus Development Corporation filed suit against Borland and SCO.[6] Dave Fulton, president of Fox Software, at the time a defendant in a copyright suit filed by Ashton-Tate, is quoted in the article as saying: "Copyrights covering the interface will reverse any trend toward uniformity. . . . It creates a legally mandated Tower of

Babel." The assumption here, of course, is that uniformity is an overriding goal, more important than encouraging innovation. If uniformity is to be the overriding goal, however, and intellectual property were to be free for the taking, where would we find the incentive for innovation that has made the United States the leader in the computing field?

As the late Alan J. Perlis, a pioneer in the computer field, once said: "The time to standardize something is when no one cares about it any longer." What he meant was that as long as people really care about something and are trying to make it better, standardization might be premature. With an industry as young and dynamic as the computer industry, we should encourage innovation and be wary of any march toward uniformity in the name of the consumer. We might achieve uniformity too soon.

NOTES

1.   Actually, the 1-2-3 product is a computer program, an application program, which displays on the user's screen a grid of cells, and a mechanism for selection of a variety of commands that the product software carries out for the user, such as putting a value in a cell, associating various attributes with that value, and so on. A particular collection of such commands, packaged into a program that controls the product in producing a specific report, for example, will be referred to here as a "spreadsheet program," but this should not be confused with the software for the 1-2-3 product itself, or any of its competitor products.

2.   Such as Microsoft (EXCEL), Borland (Quattro Pro), and Paperback Software (VP-Planner).

3.   In the latter case, the new product would be indistinguishable to the user from the established product, and the competition would be based on price and performance alone, along with promises of excellent subsequent support, such as advice, training, maintenance, and enhancements.

4.   A second company, Mosaic Software, was also sued by Lotus, and the two suits were joined, but at the trial the attorney for Mosaic was ill, and the opinion of the court was restricted to the Paperback Software case. The other case was resolved at a later date, with similar results.

5.   Bricklin, D. *Lotus Development Corp.* v. *Microsoft Corporation et al.*, 94 C.D.O.S. 7160 (9th Cir. 1994), Affdvt. pp. 176-177, 179-80.

6.   InfoWorld Staff, "Copyright Suits Could Slow Innovation," *InfoWorld* 12 (July 9, 1990): 1.

9

Reverse Engineering

The Council of the European Communities (CEC), in its Council Directive of May 14, 1991, contains the clause (Article 5 (3)): "The person having a right to use a computer program shall be entitled, without the authorization of the rightholder, to observe, study or test the functioning of the program in order to determine the ideas and principles which underlie any element of the program if he does so while performing any of the acts of loading, displaying, running, transmitting or storing the program which he is entitled to do."[1]

Such observation, study, and testing is generally referred to as "reverse engineering." As yet, there does not seem to be a more formal definition than this. Reverse engineering has probably been going on in almost every field of endeavor since the invention of the wheel, but in the last couple of years it has become a controversial practice, at least as it has been applied to computer programs. The reason that this time-honored practice has been challenged is that reverse engineering of computer programs has gone far beyond behavioral study and testing, to disassembly of the program itself.

As we shall see, disassembly of a computer program is very different from taking apart an automobile or a watch. If you disassemble a watch, you can see all of the parts and how they fit together, but you probably do not find out much about the design process that preceded its manufacture, or much about any trade secrets that may have led to an efficient manufacturing process. If you want to compete in the watch market, you will have set up your own watch factory and handle all of the up-front costs that are involved in manufacturing. The disassembly of a computer program reveals essentially all there is to know about a program. In addition, it puts the new owner in a position to very quickly begin to manufacture a competing product, with relatively little cost or time delay.

Disassembly of a computer program is the process of starting with the object code of a program, in the form of 0s and 1s, and, usually with the aid of a computer, constructing a corresponding program in assembler language for the instructions embedded in the object code. In other words, the result of disassembling a program is that same program in assembler language. If that resulting program were then translated by the assembler language processor, the resulting object code should be identical to the original object code with which the process started.[2]

The advantage of disassembling a program, for the person who wants to study the program and learn all about it, is that almost all of the original structure and computational algorithms can be gleaned from the assembler language version that results. To be sure, the original names that were used by the author are lost because they are not normally present in the object code, as well as any comments that may have been written into the original program as documentation. But with careful study, a great deal can be learned. Even more of an advantage comes from the fact that the disassembled version is still in the computer, and is subject to various kinds of analysis.

From the point of view of the original author, there are two concerns.

1. It is a trivial exercise to use the same computer to make a number of modifications to the original program, enough to make the program look quite different from the original program, but to preserve the essential characteristics. Most important among these characteristics, one can preserve the computational behavior and create a competitive product available for the market, with only a fraction of the effort needed to produce the original product. This has been done in a number of cases, leading to some well-publicized litigation.

2. With additional study, it is possible to deduce directly from the code a number of possible trade secrets, such as mathematical formulas, data structures, program and module organization, and compression and other algorithms.

There is a tension, then, between those who want to use reverse engineering to study a competitive product and those who want to restrict the use of reverse engineering, or at least the use of disassembly as part of it, to minimize the possibility of illegal copying. In part because of this tension, and because of the special nature of the process of manufacturing computer chips, Congress passed a special law, the Semiconductor Chip Protection Act (SCPA) of 1984,[3] to govern the rights and responsibilities of chip manufacturers. One of the unique aspects of this law is that it explicitly provides, in §906, for reverse engineering:

(a) It is not an infringement of the exclusive rights of the owner of a mask work[4] for —

  (1) a person to reproduce the mask work solely for the purpose of teaching, analyzing, or evaluating the concepts or techniques embodied in the mask work or the circuitry, logic flow, or organization of components used in the mask work; or
  (2) a person who performs the analysis or evaluation described in paragraph (1) to incorporate the results of such conduct in an original mask work which is made to be distributed.

(b) The owner of a particular semiconductor chip product made by the owner of the mask work, or by any person authorized by the owner of the mask work, may import, distribute, or otherwise dispose of or use, but not reproduce, that particular semiconductor chip product without the authority of the owner of the mask work.

As explained in the report from the U. S. Congress (1992) in their discussion of the SCPA:

The SCPA uses a modified copyright approach to protect the typography of integrated circuits against copying. There is no patentlike examination process; the "mask work" is registered with the Copyright Office. However, the SCPA has a novelty standard somewhat higher then the mere "originality" standard of copyright law: protection is not available for a mask work that "consists of designs that are staple, commonplace, or familiar in the semiconductor industry or variations of such designs, combined in a way that, considered as a whole, is not original" (17 U.S.C. 902(b)(2)). The bundle of rights is also somewhat different from that granted under copyright law, and copies of the "mask work" made in the course of reverse engineering are not infringing (17 U.S.C. 906(a)). Finally, semiconductor chip protection differs from copyright in that the term of protection is only 10 years. (p. 27)

The Act establishes reverse engineering as a defense to a claim of infringement. The reverse engineering provisions provide an exemption from infringement liability in spite of proof of unauthorized copying and striking similarity, as long as the resulting chip product was the result of study and analysis and contained technological improvement. The act also provides remedies similar to those associated with copyright protection. However, criminal penalties are not available, and the limit on statutory damages is higher than that provided for by the Copyright Act. (p. 76)

The use of reverse engineering as sanctioned by the SCPA was one of the issues in an important case, *Brooktree Corporation* v. *Advanced Micro Devices, Inc.* Because this was the first such case to go to the U. S. Court of Appeals in the Federal Circuit, the court took pains to explore all of the issues very carefully, and the resulting opinion lays out the reasoning completely, including the relationship between the SCPA and existing copyright and patent law. There is also an interesting discussion of reverse engineering:

In performing reverse engineering a person may disassemble, study, and analyze an existing chip in order to understand it. This knowledge may be used to create an original chip having a different design layout. . . . Congress was told by industry representatives that reverse engineering was an accepted and fair practice, . . . serving competition while advancing the state of technology.

It was explained [by a witness] that a person engaged in reverse engineering seeks to understand the design of the original chip. . . . Another witness explained that reverse engineering generally produces a "paper trail."

Whenever there is a true reverse engineering, the second firm will have prepared a great deal of paper — logic and circuit diagrams, trial layouts. . . . A pirate has no such papers, for the pirate does none of this work. Therefore, whether there has been a true reverse engineering job or just a job of copying can be shown by looking at the defendant's records.

Brooktree

Case: *Brooktree Corp.* v. *Advanced Micro Devices, Inc.*,
          977 F.2d 1555 (Fed. Cir. 1992)

Date: October 9, 1992

Original decision: 757 F.Supp. 1088 (S. D. Cal. 1990)

Summary: Brooktree brought an action against AMD for patent infringement and mask work registration infringement under the SCPA. The District Court ruled in favor of Brooktree, and this ruling was appealed. The issues before the District Court included whether an entire chip had to be copied for infringement to occur, and whether reverse engineering was a defense. AMD engineers had an extensive "paper trail" showing considerable reverse engineering effort on their part, but this extensive record was very slim after the point where they learned how Brooktree had solved a crucial problem in the design of their chip. The part that had been found to be copied was the main cell in the chip layout, replicated thousands of times. Although this did not cover the entire chip, it was a major part of the innovation in the chip's design.

Decision: The Appeals Court affirmed the original decision, finding that there had been infringement, both of the mask work and of the patent involved in the case.

The idea of a "paper trail" is not a new one. There are many situations where one might need to establish a level of effort in this way. For example, in a typical trade-secret litigation, the defendant is accused of using secrets of a former employer to create a competing product. The argument is made by the plaintiff that the new product could not have been designed and put into production, with all of the attendant documentation in the case of software, in such a short time without the use of the proprietary information that had been misappropriated by the defendant. The defense uses a paper trail to document the independent effort that went into the creation of the new product. It is not just the amount of effort that is being demonstrated, but the sequence of investigations, the mistakes that are recorded, and the reasonableness of the elapsed time for the project. In one case in which I participated,[5] the existence of a full-blown manual, as well as the product itself, and the lack of a paper trail, one month after the defendant left his former employer, was pretty convincing evidence of a trade-secret violation. Of course, the plaintiff also had to show that the other elements of trade secret law were fulfilled, including the value of the information taken, the continued treatment of that information as proprietary, and so on.

The fact that an explicit allowance of reverse engineering was built into the SCPA recognizes the tension mentioned above, as well as the lack of resolution of this tension with regard to other aspects of computer intellectual property protection, such as copyright law. Note that in the SCPA one protects an explicit circuit design on a chip, rather than possible embedded trade secrets such as complex algorithms and others mentioned earlier.

Given that there is no explicit proscription of reverse engineering or disassembly available to them, the opponents of disassembly of computer programs have resorted to copyright law to try to stop the free use of disassembly. It is clear that during any disassembly process, some kind of copy of the original program must be made. The argument is then made that the final assembler-language version of the original machine-language program is a derivative work based on the original program, thus infringing on the copyright. In any case, copyright infringement has been the argument that has been used to try to outlaw disassembly, in an attempt to reduce the apparently increasing number of illegal copies of commercial software appearing on the market, and thus protect the original investment of time, resources, and creativity.

It is unfortunate that the copyright law seems to be the only method available to resolve the disassembly conflict. At some point there will need to be a policy resolution on reverse engineering and disassembly, just as it was made explicit in the SCPA and in the CEC directive, although the result might not be the same. It seems to dilute the theory and application of the copyright form of protection to use it to head off the specific act of disassembly. If trade secrets are to be protected against reverse engineering, and if direct commercial exploitation of disassembled code is to be ruled out, this is a policy decision that Congress and the courts will have to face head-on eventually.

There have been some developments that may in the long run lead to the desired policy resolution. In the CEC Directive of 1991 mentioned above, the preamble contains their justification for allowing disassembly, based on interoperability:

Whereas, . . . circumstances may exist when such a reproduction of the code and translation of its form . . . are indispensable to obtain the necessary information to achieve the interoperability of an independently created program with other programs;

Whereas it has therefore to be considered that in these limited circumstances only, performance of the acts of reproduction and translation by or on behalf of a person having a right to use a copy of the program is legitimate and compatible with fair practice and must therefore be deemed not to require the authorization of the rightholder;

Whereas an objective of this exception is to make it possible to connect all components of a computer system, including those of different manufacturers, so that they can work together;

Whereas such an exception to the author's exclusive rights may not be used in a way which prejudices the legitimate interests of the rightholder or which conflicts with a normal exploitation of the program.

The report of the U.S. Congress (1992) mentioned earlier characterizes the adoption of the Directive as occurring "after extensive and heated debate" (p. 17). That is not surprising because the conditions under which disassembly is allowed, with the resulting risk of illegal copying, do not seem to be too restrictive. The following year there were two important legal decisions in the United States which bear on this same issue: *Sega Enterprises Ltd.* v. *Accolade, Inc.* and *Atari Games Corp.* v. *Nintendo of America, Inc.*

THE ATARI AND SEGA CASES

It is too early to tell how these two cases will shape the future, but, at present, they appear to be very important. In essence, they both move in the direction of weakening an inventor's protection against abuse in the use of reverse engineering by making it easier to argue that the disassembly that was done was allowed under the "fair use" exceptions to the rights of the inventor. Of course, if the argument is successful, and the disassembly is in fact a fair use, there is no abuse.

Atari lost in its attempt to avoid an injunction against marketing their Nintendo-compatible games, but not because of reverse engineering. Atari came into the case with "unclean hands," as the lawyers would say. After trying unsuccessfully to reverse engineer the Nintendo authorization code, Atari sent its attorney to the Copyright Office to obtain a copy of the Nintendo source code, under the guise of being involved in litigation and needing the source code for that purpose. The litigation that ensued had, in fact, not started yet.[6] In part because of this action, and because of the clear history of the process by which Atari used the source code and their reverse engineering to break Nintendo's security system, the District Court found that Nintendo had shown a likelihood of prevailing with its copyright infringement claims. As a result, an injunction was issued against Atari. The Appeals Court affirmed the injunction but decided that the lower court had erred in ruling that the use of intermediate copies in this case constituted copyright infringement. The Appeals Court reasoning was based on the doctrine of fair use.

Atari

Case: *Atari Games Corp.* v. *Nintendo of America, Inc.*,
975 F.2d 832 (Fed. Cir. 1992)

Date: September 9, 1992

Original decision: 18 U.S.P.Q.2D (BNA) 1935 (N.D. Cal. 1991)

Summary: Nintendo had devised a program, 10NES, which would stop unauthorized game cartridges from working with its console. Atari tried to decipher the information that passed between the cartridge and the console, in order to market games that would work with the console. They wanted to bypass a license arrangement with Nintendo. Failing to determine the necessary information by reverse engineering, Atari obtained a copy of the Nintendo source code from the Copyright Office by subterfuge, and was then able to use this information to duplicate the program needed to authorize their cartridges to work with the Nintendo console. The issue of interest here was their use of reverse engineering and whether it was appropriately a fair use.

Decision: The Appeals Court affirmed the District Court's preliminary injunction against Atari, although it did rule that the reverse engineering that Atari did was a fair use of disassembly of the object code.

FAIR USE

Although entire books have been written on the doctrine of fair use,[7] this section will only outline the basic ideas, so that the application of fair use in the context of reverse engineering will be understood.

Copyright law reserves to an author a number of rights, as we have seen. On the other hand, the public interest benefits from wide dissemination of creative works. Toward this end, there are some limitations on authors' rights. The exclusive rights given to authors are in §106 of the Copyright Act, while the limitations are in §107–120. In particular, while original expression is protected, society is free to use facts, ideas, processes, or methods of operation embedded in a copyrighted work.[8] Moreover, §107 of the Copyright Act states, as quoted in the Atari opinion, that "'fair use of a copyrighted work, including such use by reproduction in copies . . . for purposes such as criticism, comment, news reporting, teaching . . . scholarship or research' is not infringement. 17 U.S.C. §107. The legislative history of section 107 suggests that courts should adapt the fair use exception to accommodate new technological innovations."

As described in the report from the U. S. Congress (1992, p. 62 [footnote omitted]):

It has been said that the doctrine of "fair use" allows the courts to bypass an inflexible application of copyright law, when under certain circumstances it would impede the creative activity that the copyright law was supposed to stimulate. Indeed, some commentators have viewed the flexibility of the doctrine as the "safety valve" of copyright law, especially in times of rapid technological change. Others have considered the uncertainties of the fair-use doctrine the source of unresolved ambiguities.

In codifying the fair-use exception in the Copyright Act of 1976, Congress did not formulate a specific test for determining whether a particular use was to be construed as a fair use. Rather, Congress created statutory recognition of a list of factors that courts should consider in making their fair-use determinations. The four factors set out in the statute are:

1. the purpose and character of the use, including whether such use is of a commercial nature or is for nonprofit educational purposes;

2. the nature of the copyrighted work;

3. the amount and substantiality of the portion used in relation to the copyrighted work as a whole; and

4. the effect of the use on the potential market and value of the copyrighted work (17 U.S.C. 107 (1988)).[9]

The Atari Appeals Court struggled with Atari's copying of Nintendo's work, regarding it as infringement unless it came under the fair-use exception: "Fair use to discern a work's ideas . . . does not justify extensive efforts to profit from replicating protected expression. . . . Fair use in intermediate copying does not extend to commercial exploitation of protected expression. . . . The fair use reproductions of a computer program must not exceed what is necessary to understand the unprotected elements of the work. This limited exception is not an invitation to misappropriate protectable expression." Having said this, the court went on to allow Atari to disassemble Nintendo's code under the fair use doctrine, notwithstanding its commercial purpose:

Reverse engineering . . . is a fair use. An individual cannot even observe, let alone understand, the object code on Nintendo's chip without reverse engineering. . . . Atari engineers transcribed the 10NES object code into a handwritten list . . . [that] convey[s] little, if any, information to the normal unaided observer. Atari then keyed this handwritten copy into a computer. The computer "disassembled" the object code or otherwise aided the observer in understanding the program's method or functioning. This "reverse engineering" process . . . qualified as a fair use. . . . This fair use did not give Atari more than the right to understand the 10NES program and to distinguish the protected from the unprotected elements of the 10NES program. Any copying beyond that necessary to understand the 10NES program was infringement. Atari could not use reverse engineering as an excuse to exploit commercially or otherwise misappropriate protected expression.

It is a little difficult to see where there was no commercial exploitation by Atari in this case. This factor could have been given much more weight than the court gave it.

Sega

Case: *Sega Enterprises Ltd.* v. *Accolade, Inc.,*
             977 F.2d 1510 (9th Cir. 1992)

Date: January 6, 1993

Original decision: 785 F.Supp. 1392 (N.D.Cal. 1992)

Summary: Sega incorporated into its game cartridges a sequence of
             characters that were transmitted to the Sega console, which
             recognized the sequence and then allowed the cartridge to
             work with the console. Accolade used reverse engineering
             to discover the exact sequence of four characters needed to
             be communicated to the console, and thus was enabled to
             create game cartridges that could be marketed as compatible
             with Sega consoles. Accolade was able to avoid getting a
             restrictive license from Sega. The main issue of interest here
             was whether reverse engineering was a fair use of the work,
             which might otherwise be copyright infringement.

Decision: The Appeals Court reversed the District Court's preliminary
             injunction against Accolade, which had been based on
             copyright infringement, allowing them to continue to
             market their games. Other issues were sent back to the
             District Court for further consideration.

On September 1, 1992, reporter Junda Woo of *The Wall Street Journal*
wrote: "A soon-to-be published appeals court decision apparently will let
software makers take apart rival companies' products to see how they
work. The decision is expected to be an important victory for computer-
program developers. . . . Proponents of reverse engineering say that
forcing every program designer to begin at ground level discourages
innovation in software and makes software more expensive." Reverse
engineering was never the real issue in these cases, however. Reverse
engineering has always been accepted, even with regard to software, as
long as the goal has been to discover ideas. The new issues introduced
into the software arena by the Atari and Sega cases revolved around the
use of disassembly as part of the reverse engineering. The Sega Appeals
Court also relied on fair use to determine that the use of disassembly by
Accolade was permissible.

The Sega Appeals Court opinion is clearly written and well reasoned, but I might have reached a different conclusion in this case, and I shall make my concern clear as I proceed.

First, as the court pointed out: "Accolade is not and never has been a licensee of Sega. Prior to rendering its own games compatible with [Sega's] Genesis console, Accolade explored the possibility of entering into a licensing agreement with Sega, but abandoned the effort because the agreement would have required that Sega be the exclusive manufacturer of all games produced by Accolade."

In other words, Accolade decided that it did not like the license offered by Sega. The court did not mention Accolade's decision again, and in fact, many courts have ruled that the availability of a license is not relevant in deciding whether the use of another's work is fair or not. The reasoning is that if the action is legal, as in a legitimate fair use, one should not have to consider paying for the right to do it. The legality of the action should be determined first. If the action is illegal, then maybe the fact that a license would have been available could be taken into account as evidence that the infringement was willful.

Second, the court determined that: "Although the question is fairly debatable, we conclude based on the policies underlying the Copyright Act that disassembly of copyrighted object code is, as a matter of law, a fair use of the copyrighted work if such disassembly provides the only means of access to those elements of the code that are not protected by copyright and the copier has a legitimate reason for seeking such access."

There are two conditions, then, that the court says are necessary to justify disassembly of copyrighted code as a fair use: no other means of access to non-protected elements and a legitimate reason. With regard to the first reason, the court stated: "The need to disassemble object code arises, if at all, only in connection with operations [sic] systems, system interface procedures, and other programs that are not visible to the user when operating — and then only when no alternative means of gaining an understanding of those ideas and functional concepts exists." But then the Court went on to reason that "the record clearly establishes that disassembly of the object code in Sega's video game cartridges was necessary in order to understand the functional requirements for Genesis compatibility. . . . Because object code cannot be read by humans, it must be disassembled. . . . If disassembly of copyrighted object code is per se an unfair use, the owner of the copyright gains a de facto monopoly over the functional aspects of his work — aspects that were expressly denied copyright protection by Congress."

The latter part of this argument is similar to the merger argument. If there is no other way to get to a legitimate goal, copyright protection should not be allowed to stand in the way. Where I differ is in the technical statement that, "because object code cannot be read by humans, it must be disassembled." What Accolade needed was the information contained in 20 to 25 bytes of code plus the characters S, E, G, and A. It would seem that reverse engineering short of disassembly would suffice to recognize the data stream thus generated between the game cartridge and the console. If that is correct, then disassembly would not be justified.

With regard to the second condition, the legitimate reason, the court determined that there was an overriding public interest to justify Accolade's actions: "Accolade's identification of the functional requirements for Genesis compatibility has led to an increase in the number of independently designed video game programs offered for use with the Genesis console. It is precisely this growth in creative expression, based on the dissemination of other creative works and the unprotected ideas contained in those works, that the Copyright Act was intended to promote."

Of course, if Accolade had obtained the license, the public availability of Accolade's games would also have been promoted, albeit through a business arrangement with Sega. As indicated above, however, once it was determined that Accolade's action was a fair use, the availability of the license was not relevant. When the use is indeed fair, there is no reason for payment for the right to do it.

The bottom line, it seems, is that there should be little reason, based on these cases, for rejoicing by those who are seeking unlimited access to copyrighted code using disassembly. The arguments of the Sega court are sufficiently close, and the circumstances sufficiently unique, that it may take additional cases to sharpen the issue, if not a Supreme Court opinion.

THE JAPANESE INITIATIVE

In 1993 it was learned that the Japanese government was considering a modification of their copyright law to allow unlimited disassembly. As expressed by at least one proponent of this change, the goal is "preventing redundant investments in similar technologies."[10] Apparently in answer to strong criticism of this proposed change, the Japanese government formed a group to review the issue, which they called the Collaborators' Council. This group convened a hearing at which a number of industrial and academic representatives were invited to present their views. I presented the following testimony:[11]

Alternatives to Disassembly in the Study of Computer Programs

A recent Court opinion, in *Sega* v. *Accolade*, stated that "disassembly of the object code . . . was necessary in order to understand the functional requirements for . . . compatibility." At another point in the opinion, however, the Court stated: ". . . where disassembly is the only way to gain access to the ideas and functional elements embodied in a copyrighted computer program and where there is a legitimate reason for seeking such access, disassembly is a fair use of the copyrighted work."

There is an important difference between these two statements. The first refers to the functional requirements for compatibility, or in this context *interoperability*. The second refers to the "ideas and functional elements embodied in a copyrighted computer program," which are not protected under the Copyright Act. The Court did not distinguish between interface specifications needed for interoperability, and internal "ideas and functional elements," almost all of which are not needed for interoperability. There is a great difference between the two concepts, and disassembly of machine-readable code is not necessary for either one. In particular, "access to the ideas and functional elements embodied in a copyrighted computer program" is in fact undesirable from an engineering point of view, for all parties concerned with software development for interoperability. On the other hand, disassembly "solely" to achieve interoperability where "necessary in order to understand the functional requirements for . . . compatibility" has superficial appeal. But, as I shall show below, it can only be justified based on an incorrect technical assumption: that no other technical approach to achieve interoperability is available.

In the following, I shall refer to the object whose interface specifications we wish to determine as the *target object*, and the product to be developed as the *compatible object*.

For a competitor who is seeking interoperability, it is actually much better, from an engineering point of view, to stay away from detailed information on the low-level sequence and structure of a target program. This strategy lowers the potential for inadvertent copying of sequence and structure, and avoids the inclusion in the interface of unnecessary structure that may change in future enhancements of the target product.

The general principle, which I have often heard referred to as "The Principle of Hiding," is that neither party on opposite sides of an interface should know what is being done on the other side of the interface, so that either party is free to change the technology, algorithms, or data structures on its side without fear of affecting the other.[12] The immediate benefit from the application of this principle is that both parties can make continuous improvements, even drastic changes, with freedom. This is a principle which I have emphasized in my teaching for many years.

The basis of the Court's approval of otherwise infringing actions for compatibility purposes was the absence of evidence that there were alternate ways to determine the requirements for interoperability. In the following I shall explore methods of obtaining such interoperability information without disassembly.

At the outset, I should note that we have available to us not only the target object with which we want to interoperate, but some examples that are already compatible with it. In the case of a game cartridge, we have access to the game console as well as a number of cartridges. In the more general case, we would have the program disk containing the application program, as well as the host system, and so on. There is in fact a well-defined interface between the compatible examples mentioned above and the target product.

Of course, disassembly is attractive to some people, since it is quite easily accomplished, and it yields far more information than is necessary for interoperability. In fact, once a disassembled version of a program is available, one could with trivial changes disguise substantial portions of the code and use them illegally with relative impunity in competing products.

To appreciate the unfair advantage gained by disassembling code, assume that a typical language processor has about 36,000 lines of code in some high-level language. A well-known, and remarkably stable rule of thumb in the software industry is that professional programmers will, on the average, produce 10 lines of correct code per day (in any language) over the entire development life cycle of a product.[13] For this illustration, then, the effort to produce the language processor would be 3,600 man/days. If a competitor wanted to produce a competing product independently, the descriptive material available publicly for the original product, and observations of its behavior under use, might shorten the problem specification time by 80%. Since another industry-accepted rule of thumb allocates about one-fifth of the overall development life cycle to the problem specification, the competitor would save, legally, 80% of one-fifth of the effort, 576 man/days.

Now suppose that the competitor assigns one of its programming experts to the task of disassembling the original product and then disguising the result so that it would appear to be an independent effort. A poor job of disguising the disassembled result, such as a student might do, would take a couple of days; an expert job perhaps two weeks, including debugging. Not much debugging would have to be done, since the only errors to be eliminated would be those introduced during the disguising effort. Conservatively, let us assume that the effort to disguise the disassembled code takes as much as 60 man/days. That represents less than 2% of the effort put into the original product, and also of the effort the competitor would have had to put into its product legally. This makes the disassembly route very attractive.

I have seen on many occasions in my teaching activities at the University of Michigan the results of excessive cooperation among students. Just as disassembly makes the results of one party's creative efforts easily available to another, the use by one student of another's work, with or without permission, is reprehensible. We often find such examples, even in a class of several hundred students. Truly independent work in software development is a creative activity, and the resulting expression of the ideas involved typically depends on thousands of choices. Different people will make those choices very differently, and that is what gives the software industry its great potential for innovation. When there is too much cooperation, such as when students collaborate, or when one party disassembles another's code, this innovation is truly stifled. That is why we can recognize when students do cooperate too much, and why the courts recognize access and substantial similarity as evidence of copying. On the other hand, as the illustration just given shows, it is worthwhile for a competitor to invest quite a lot in disguising the result of disassembly, since it represents such a small fraction of the otherwise required creative effort.

Going now to the interface specification, the basic idea of an interface is that information must be communicated in both directions. If one could determine what information is communicated under all relevant circumstances, that would specify the interface. It would be very helpful if the writer of the source code and/or the interface specifications gave them to us in the form in which they are known to him. Thus, the first and most desirable source of information is the vendor of the software in question. It is almost always in the interest of the vendor to make such information available, perhaps by license, since this usually results in more software on the market that can be used with the original product, and thus improves the vendor's position in the marketplace.

If information is not available from the vendor, one must establish a table of relevant input sequences, such as electrical signals or bit strings, that would go across the interface toward the target, and relevant responses and other observable behavior, such as screen presentations, alarm signals, etc., that follow on the part of the target. To this end, we may assume that the relevant communication across the interface occurs between two software modules running on the same hardware, or between software modules residing on different hardware platforms and communicating across a network link or, as in the case of a cartridge, a direct hardware connection. In either case, it is not difficult to create a monitoring device of some kind, involving some combination of hardware and/or software, that can detect and log all communication across the boundary between the target object and the compatible object. If necessary, one could intercede after each communication event and study the contents of the memory on each machine involved, or even after each instruction is executed. Methods for doing such monitoring are well known in the industry. Observable behavior, such as screen presentations, etc., can also be logged by a human observer while running experiments based on the use of the compatible examples.

In each case, the information that crosses the boundary will be either (1) data, (2) system calls, i.e., jumps into an operating system or other application modules requesting service, or (3) program segments that would be executed on the target computer once they came across the boundary, with the last very rarely used:

(1) Data: If data is being communicated, it is relatively easy to log the actual data over a period of time and compare it across several compatible examples to detect patterns.

(2) System calls: System calls, or more generally requests for service from either the operating system or another application module, can be detected during a monitoring session. They may take the form of conventional "branch-and-link" instructions, or direct "go-to" instructions. In either case, the request will result in some response or observable behavior on the part of the target, which can be logged. Having compatible examples available should make it possible to experiment with a variety of requests while observing the resulting behavior of the target.

(3) Program Segments: If it is discovered that actual code is being communicated across the interface, a rare event, it would be necessary to know enough about the architecture of the target computer to be able to understand the nature of the communicated program segments and to generate code which is compatible with that computer. The information

needed would include the instruction set, the nature of any peripherals that might be involved in the interface, timing restrictions, and so on. If the architecture is well known and public, that makes the task easier. If not, then testing can be performed to determine the requirements of those program segments which would be communicated to the target computer.

I note that we do not need to know everything about the architecture, or for that matter, everything about the interface. *We need to know only that which is necessary for interoperability.* There may be aspects of the interface, the architecture, or the code on either side of the interface that will never be known, but that are irrelevant to the interoperability requirement, since they would never be invoked while using the compatible object and the target object together. The Principle of Hiding mentioned earlier suggests that it is in fact a good thing not to know more than is needed to understand the interface.

How will we know when we have learned enough about the interface? What is enough? We can define "enough" in terms of the compatible object to be developed. We are in control of the design of the compatible object, and we can determine the scope of its desired behavior. In other words, we can specify precisely the amount of testing that has to be done to determine if the compatible object works correctly. If it must work in conjunction with the target object, then the testing must be done on a system consisting of both the compatible object and the target object. If the combination works according to the specification of the compatible object, then enough is known about the interface, and the job is done.

A final observation: There is a distinct difference between reverse engineering and disassembly. Disassembly is just one of many tools that are available for reverse engineering. All of the alternate methods of finding information about an interface mentioned above are included in the concept of reverse engineering, and they are legitimate methods under current law. The argument here is not against reverse engineering, but against the use of disassembly as part of that process.

To summarize, there are a number of legal tools available for effectively reverse engineering (i.e., obtaining information about) an interface, some of which I have discussed, and some of which, such as tracing the execution of instructions on both sides of the interface, have not been mentioned here. These tools are legal and effective, but more time-consuming than disassembly. Although some find that it is attractive to advocate the free use of disassembly of machine-readable code, disassembly is not necessary, nor even desirable, for interoperability.

The Wall Street Journal reported about a month after the Collaborators' Council hearing that the Japanese government had postponed a decision on the proposed change in their copyright law. On May 19, 1994, it was reported in the Ann Arbor News that the advisory committee to the Agency for Cultural Affairs, presumably the Collaborators' Council, had completed their deliberations without reporting out any recommendations, and that this most likely meant that no change would be made in the Japanese copyright law.

NOTES

1. "Council Directive of May 14, 1991, on the legal protection of computer programs," amended October 29, 1993.
2. Some people use the term decompilation instead of disassembly for this process, but most computer people reserve decompilation for the process of going from object code to some higher-level language. Going to a higher-level language is a much more complicated process, and there are no generally available tools for doing it, while there are many disassembler processors on the market.
3. 17 U.S.C. 901 *et seq.*
4. A mask work is an image or template used to create the circuitry on a computer chip.
5. *Squibb Corporation.* v. *Diagnostic Medical Instruments, Inc.*, Civ. Act. 83-CV-712 (N. D. New York), October 21, 1983.
6. As noted in the Appeals Court opinion:

In 1991, the Copyright Office circulated the following notice:
The Copyright Office has recently become aware that an attorney completing the previous Litigation Statement form provided by the Office could generally allege that a controversy existed when in fact no real controversy did exist. An attorney could thus receive reproductions of deposits not authorized by the regulations. The Litigation Statement form has been amended to require the applicant to give more specific information regarding prospective proceedings and to include supporting documentation. (56 Fed. Reg. 12,957 (1991)).

7. See, for example, Paltry [1985].
8. See 17 USC §102.
9. I note that these four factors are not intended in the statute to be exclusive.
10. September 27, 1993, report of the Working Group on Protection of Computer Programs, Japan Federation of Economic Organizations (Keidanren), Majority opinion, at paragraph 1.1(a).
11. December 18, 1993, Tokyo, Japan
12. This was formulated by David L. Parnas in "On the Criteria to be Used in Decomposing Systems into Modules," *Communications of the ACM*, December 1972, pp. 1053–58.
13. The software development life cycle includes problem specification, solution design, coding, integration, and debugging of the product. The rules of thumb mentioned here were discussed in Brooks (1975).

REFERENCES

Brooks, F. P., Jr., *The Mythical Man-Month* (Reading, Mass.: Addison-Wesley, 1975).

Paltry, William, *The Fair Use Privilege in Copyright Law* (Washington, D.C.: The Bureau of National Affairs, 1985).

U.S. Congress, Office of Technology Assessment, *Finding a Balance: Computer Software, Intellectual Property, and the Challenge of Technological Change*, OTA-TCT-527 (Washington, D.C.: U.S. Government Printing Office, 1992).

10

The Clean Room Approach

The term "clean room" is not new. It refers to an environment, and a process carried out within that environment, in which there is a concerted effort to avoid even the slightest contamination. Although similar to the "Chinese Wall" in the legal profession, the use of the clean room to avoid copyright infringement allegations in the software field is quite new. In fact, it appears that no court has, to date, explicitly written on the rules for the use of the clean room in the computer field, and there are no decisions as yet that would serve as a guide for implementing a successful clean room in the computer field.[1] Nevertheless, the clean room concept, if done correctly, can be advantageously employed to avoid litigation or as a defense in litigation between computer companies.

The clean room is most likely to be of use to avoid charges of copyright infringement or as a defense in copyright litigation.[2] Given a copyrightable product, a competitor is faced with the option of attempting to obtain a license from the owner of the copyright for the use of the original product or deciding to generate its own expression of the idea involved using only publicly available information and its own original writing. In the latter case, there is still the risk in the future of possible allegations of copyright infringement by the owner of the copyright. The clean room is a mechanism for providing the competitor with the basis for a defense by demonstrating that its product was independently developed. In other words, there could not have been access to the original product by the people isolated in the clean room, so there could not have been copying.

Although no format for a clean room has been challenged or tested in court, a clean room will only be effective if certain basic guidelines for setting up a clean room are followed as carefully as possible or practical.

In a typical situation, Origin Software, Inc. has on the market a popular application program (which will be referred to as the Program), and competitor Follower Software, Inc. decides to market its own version.[3] The marketing arm of Follower has determined that a strong market exists for software that mirrors (exactly, if possible) the external behavior of Origin's Program. It is well known, however, that Origin has been diligently protecting its copyright on Program. Because the external characteristics of Program are publicly available, the management of Follower decides to set up a clean room to avoid later charges by Origin of copyright infringement. Under this arrangement, Follower will attempt to establish that its software developers have had access only to the public description of the features and functionality of Program. If it is successful in establishing and maintaining careful control over its clean room, Follower may be able to argue successfully at a later time that the code it generated was independently developed. If that can be done, there can be no conclusion of copying, even if there is later seen to be substantial similarity between the products. Substantial similarity is only an argument in favor of copying when coupled with access, and the clean room is used precisely to argue against the possibility of access.

How does Follower go about setting up a clean room? What are the pitfalls and inadvertent oversights that would destroy the credibility of the process and leave the company still exposed to possible suspicion of copying? To put it in a more positive framework, what are the appropriate guidelines for establishing a clean room that would leave no doubt as to the non-infringing nature of the resulting product? How can one demonstrate independent development?

Essentially, only non-protected information can be used. Anyone familiar with the original Program should have nothing to do with the clean room project or with the people involved, and all activity should be recorded and thoroughly documented to show the entire process of development. Here are specific guidelines:

1.   The occupants of the clean room should have had no access to the source code in question, or to any design documents or other information that could suggest how the original creator of the software organized, modularized, or parametrized the software. Former employees of, or independent contractors to, the company that developed the target software should not be included in the clean room because they may be

familiar with many software-development conventions and practices that might inadvertently be reproduced in the clean room design and/or code.

2. The physical location of the clean room activity should discourage, even eliminate, communication between the occupants and other people who might have had contact with the copyrighted code or its related design documents and procedures. While it may place a burden on the occupants, social contact, such as at parties, should be avoided during the period of clean room activity. Locating the clean room physically at some distance from possible social contacts would assist in controlling this potential flaw in the clean room design.

3. A credible person or organization should act as the monitor (or filter) for all information passed into the clean room to assure that only public information is introduced. It would be best to engage a reputable independent consultant or other third party for this purpose, since control of the information that is allowed into the clean room is crucial to the ultimate credibility of the result.[4] Any information about the original software such as module designations, names of variables, file layouts, code segments, or even questions suggesting possible pitfalls to be avoided, should not be allowed to enter the clean room because of its potential influence on the organization and structure, if not the detail, of the new software being written.

4. Complete and accurate records should be kept of all information allowed into and out of the clean room, and citations should be noted at the time for each new item, attesting to its public nature. Even seemingly innocuous information, which could turn out to have been proprietary to Origin, could influence much of the design of the new Follower program and taint the entire procedure.

5. All communication between the clean room occupants and anyone else should pass through the monitor for assessment, and should be retained, either on paper, on audio or video tape, or in machine-readable form. There should be no unrecorded telephone conversations, for example, even on minor matters, such as hotel reservations. There is always the suspicion that other information may have been passed, or leading questions raised.

6. Complete records of day-to-day activity — design diagrams and specifications, user documentation, file and screen layouts, modularization plans, code segments, debugging run printouts, error corrections, and hours worked — should be retained within the clean room, carefully dated and attributed. There is no better evidence of independent development than such daily activity records.

7. The program generated in the clean room should not be seen and/or evaluated outside the clean room before the end of the activity. Another employee of Follower might be concerned if there is any similarity to Program and might attempt to influence the occupants to do the work differently.

Although some of these guidelines may appear to be obvious and simple common sense, parties attempting to employ the clean room have not always followed them. In the example described below, a party in a recent case violated virtually every guideline discussed here. The opponent chose not to make the deficiencies of the clean room an issue in the case because the results seemed to have favored its own arguments. Nevertheless, the shortcomings of the clean room setup described below should be informative for those contemplating establishing a clean room.

This case does not exactly follow the pattern outlined earlier. As we shall see, the intent here is to show that software developed independently can indeed be very similar, thus supporting a merger argument.

Company P, the plaintiff, charged Company D, the defendant, with copyright infringement with regard to certain software. In response, D argued the merger defense: for the particular software in question to run in a computer with the specific architecture under consideration, there would be so few ways to "express the solution" that the expression would merge with the idea. In other words, D argued that there was only one way, or only a few ways, to write the software, so its development of the program did not constitute infringement.

To demonstrate that the merger concept was applicable in this particular case, D set up a clean room in which an expert, referred to here as the "clean room occupant" or occupant, was given the specifications for the architecture and for the particular problem to be solved by the desired software. The occupant then wrote the software based only on the information provided. D then argued in court that the result was so similar to D's allegedly infringing software that the merger argument was clear. No matter how isolated the effort was, the resulting software would be substantially similar to D's software, and the expression would be merged with the idea.

In fact, the clean room set up by D violated almost every one of the guidelines listed above. It could have been challenged on many counts, had P chosen to do so. Here are some of their guideline violations:

Although the occupant was not a D employee, he was a former student of D's primary expert witness, and a close friend of an attorney who was a consultant for D in the current litigation. The occupant was retained on recommendation by this consultant. It could be argued that the occupant was not an entirely independent third party.

The monitor for the clean room was a member of the law firm acting as counsel for D in the case. Again, the monitor was not an entirely independent third party.

The description of the system architecture, which in some places appeared to P to contain more helpful detail than was necessary or appropriate, was written by the consultant and the monitor, and then passed on to the occupant inside the clean room. In the process of writing the specification for the software to be developed, questions raised by the consultant and the monitor were fielded by the person employed by D who allegedly copied the software in the first place. Access by this person to P's original software had been admitted by D.

During the clean room activity, when the clean room occupant needed a question answered, the consultant often answered it (through the monitor, who did keep accurate records of all such communications), but the consultant also often asked the original writer for advice.

About half-way through the activity period, when the occupant provided a first version of the new software, the consultant, with advice from the alleged copier, changed the architecture specification dramatically, apparently in an effort to force the software written by the occupant to be modified in a favorable way. Throughout the entire period of activity, changes to the architecture specification, described as corrections and/or clarifications, were passed to the occupant through the monitor.

While he was still involved with the clean room project, the occupant met socially, outside the clean room, on two occasions with people associated with D's software development work. The occupant later testified that nothing of substance relating to the clean room was discussed.

The occupant had several unrecorded telephone conversations with D employees while doing clean room work. He later had to testify that these conversations only dealt with logistics, such as payment of bills, delivery of equipment, etc.

The occupant was supplied with software debugging tools developed by the original writer. The occupant later had to testify that these tools did not influence his design or code writing.

On several occasions a messenger delivered equipment from the consultant directly to the clean room occupant and carried written messages from the occupant back to the consultant. No record was kept of conversations among the occupant, the consultant, and the messenger. The occupant was asked to testify later that no conversations of substance occurred.

Apparent similarities can occur even when programs are developed independently. Using the clean room can perhaps demonstrate the innocent development of such similar results. But where, as in this case, the process is arguably no longer credible, the clean room, at best, may be a waste of resources, and at worst may reinforce the suspicion of actual copying.

A successful use of the clean room was carried out by Phoenix Technologies, Inc. in 1984. For its Personal Computer (PC), IBM openly published much of the operating system source code. The idea was to attract software publishers to develop application software compatible with the PC operating system. The one restriction that IBM vigorously enforced was that the code for the Basic Input/Output System (BIOS) was not to be copied. IBM was willing to license the code, but it was not willing to give the code away. On a number of occasions, still continuing, IBM instituted litigation when it was necessary to stop hardware vendors from marketing copies of the BIOS code. These hardware vendors were manufacturing PC clones which were intended to mimic exactly the behavior of the PC (and its successor versions), and each of them needed a BIOS to assure compatibility to owners of existing application software. The reason that a fair amount of copying was carried out was that it was not easy to develop independently code that would provide real compatibility with the complex BIOS software. It was far easier just to copy the IBM BIOS code, if one could get away with it.

Because IBM was vigorous in its defense of its copyright on the BIOS code, Phoenix did invest in the higher cost of running a clean room operation to create their compatible version of BIOS. IBM has recognized that legitimate effort, and now other vendors are licensing the code from Phoenix as well as from IBM. It is clear that when a clean room development is done in a convincing way, it can be successful.

While the clean room concept has not been tested in court, I expect it to be an effective device in the computer field, especially if it is created in advance and with appropriate care to avoid suspicion of infringement. Companies utilizing the clean room should make every effort to follow the guidelines listed above, because failure to establish an untainted environment may defeat the entire purpose of the endeavor.

NOTES

1.   In a few cases, evidence derived from the use of a clean room has been used in court, but the rules for the organization and operation of the clean room were not an

issue in the court's decision.

2.   Note that the concept of a clean room is applicable to copyright situations, where the idea is to show that copying could not have occurred, but it would not apply to patent cases, where the legal proscription against use of the patented invention is absolute, even when there is independent development.

3.   We shall cast this example in the context of protection of source code, although it could be applied to other protected aspects of a computer product, such as the user interface, or the structure, sequence, and organization of the original product.

4.   The company should probably protect itself by asking the monitor to sign a non-disclosure agreement.

11

Where Are We Now?

It is dangerous to make predictions, especially with regard to such a rapidly changing field as computers and intellectual property. A number of very recent cases have raised issues that were thought to have been fairly well settled, such as the criticism in the Altai case of the Whelan criteria for substantial similarity based on "structure, sequence, and organization." Generally speaking, however, there has been a growing acceptance of well-known legal structures and principles as applied to the new field of computers and intellectual property. Some still argue that a whole new body of law is needed, but that does not seem to be supported by most participants in the field.

Copyright law specific to the computer field has not settled down completely in areas that have to do with the user interface and, more generally, the search for the so-called "bright line" that will separate the idea from the expression. It does not seem that this will be easy to come by in such a complex discipline as computing. A case-by-case approach will probably last a number of years, until enough precedents have been generated to cover most situations. One rule may never cover all cases automatically.

In the patent field, the advent of software-related patents has created a somewhat chaotic situation. There is hope that the efforts of the U.S. Patent & Trademark Office (PTO) to automate its own patent database to facilitate searches, plus the work of the newly created Software Patent Institute, will help the PTO do an even better job. Some possible changes are listed here.

REFORM OF THE PATENT SYSTEM

An Advisory Commission for Patent Law Reform was established by the United States Secretary of Commerce to examine the patent system in its entirety, with a view to possible reforms. The Software Patent Institute, which was specifically recognized and encouraged in their August 1992 report, has been established, as mentioned earlier, and is rapidly expanding its database. More information about the institute, about joining it, and/or contributing to the database, may be obtained by writing to the Software Patent Institute, 2901 Hubbard Street, Ann Arbor, Michigan 48105-2467.

One source of confusion in this area is the exclusion of "mathematical algorithms" from patent protection. The origin of this exclusion seems to be in the desire to avoid requests to patent the fundamental laws of nature, and perhaps of mathematics itself. No one would argue with this. But perhaps it would have been better to have simply expressed the restriction in those terms, rather than try to categorize such fundamental laws as mathematical algorithms. For one thing, it is hard to find anyone who understands what a mathematical algorithm is, much less find two people who will agree. Algorithms are processes, some of which are mathematical in nature, in that the objects they deal with have mathematical attributes, and their relationships are best expressed in the language of mathematics. That does not mean that they are fundamental laws, or that they should not be protected. Most algorithms deal with information, and although some courts apparently have found that the manipulation of bits in a computer makes an algorithm mathematical, this seems hardly appropriate to consideration of the algorithm itself. It is, in the author's opinion, the wrong test to apply here.

The purpose of a definition, in general, is to separate objects into two categories: those that satisfy the definition and those that do not. If this separation is useful and leads to intelligent discussion and action, the definition is a wise one, and if not, its use should be discouraged. The definition of mathematical algorithm appears to have been unwise because it does not separate algorithms into two classes that are useful for further discussion in the patent context, nor is it even generally understood. A more useful statement of the law would be to simply allow patents on algorithms, when justified by the usual criteria, except when the inventor appears to be attempting to patent a fundamental law of nature. One would expect the courts to have an easier time deciding on those than on mathematical algorithms.

A useful byproduct of this simplification would be that patent lawyers would not have to go to great lengths to disguise a true software algorithm as being somehow embodied in a machine. To try to make claims about a truly intellectual, abstract algorithm by describing it as a mechanical gadget of some kind only confuses the examiners (which some critics charge is the purpose of such disguise) and everyone else who must later interpret the claims. Such a simplification of the law would make the application process, as well as the approval process, much more straightforward. It would most likely help to reduce the number of inappropriately issued patents as well, thus contributing to the solution of some of the problems described earlier. An interesting and very helpful statement along these lines is the concurring opinion by Judge Rader in the case *In re Alappat* (see Appendix C).

Alappat

Case: *In re Alappat,*
             33 F.3d 1526 (Fed. Cir. 1994)

Date: July 29, 1994

Earlier decision: April 22, 1992

Summary: Alappat had applied for a patent on a technique for smoothing pixel data as it is displayed on a digital oscilloscope. Some of the claims in the patent application were rejected, primarily because they appeared to refer to a mathematical algorithm, which the examiner would not allow. A three-member panel reversed the decision, and an expanded eight-member panel reversed that decision.

Decision: The court affirmed the patentability of a software algorithm, as long as it is controlling a machine or causing a physical result.

Two types of benefits should follow from the protection of intellectual property: rewards for the inventor or author and public disclosure and availability so others can share in the progress that the invention or newly copyrighted work represents. Those who oppose patent protection for software often cite as their concern the withholding of permission to use the invention, thus impeding progress, for example, toward the establishment of conventions and standards useful to the public. There is some merit to these concerns. Although examples of this kind of abuse are not too easy to come by, the potential is there. It would be beneficial to everyone if the two types of benefits could be separated; that is, provide for rewards for an author or inventor, while making sure that the public has access to the invention — even competitors.

In another direction, it has been suggested that perhaps there should be a new kind of protection, different from both copyright protection and patent protection. It would protect only the actual code and include early disclosure, a shorter period of protection, and other features intended to alleviate some of the ills perceived in the current system. Whatever features are being suggested that may be useful considerations in the ongoing patent reform discussions, the suggestion that somehow copyright and patent protection should be merged into a single form of protection does not appear to be useful.

There has been and continues to be a legal distinction between the idea, that is, the algorithm, and its expression. In the software field there has been such a distinction since the early history of the field. Computer scientists and practitioners have long talked about the algorithm, or the abstract process by which a problem can be solved, and a specific expression of that algorithm in the form of a computer program. That distinction has been useful. The terms and the ideas that they express have been in use for almost 50 years, even as the computer field has changed dramatically. It would seem that these two levels of abstraction deserve different kinds of protection, and that copyright and patent protection are just about right. One can tune them, as suggested above, but one should not throw out the useful baby with the rejected bath water. It should be possible to make better sense of the legal system already established, which has proven useful for so many years in so many diverse fields.

I have not considered here the international ramifications of software intellectual property issues. Discussions, which have been under way for some time, are intended to lead to harmonization of United States patent laws with those of many other countries. Such harmonization has largely been accomplished for copyrights, with the adoption of the Berne convention by the United States in 1989. Discussions on patent law harmonization are continuing, however. If the conventions on patents used in most other countries are adopted, as recommended in the report of the Advisory Commission on Patent Law Reform, one very important change would occur that should have a significant impact on the processing of software-related patent applications. Instead of complete secrecy during the years needed for evaluation and approval of a patent application, the existence of the patent application — indeed, the entire application — would be published approximately 18 months into the process. This would allow significant challenges to be raised to patent applications, if appropriate, before they are officially stamped with PTO approval and would give sufficient warning to potential infringers to modify their products and/or processes so as to avoid infringement.

The PTO has taken some steps toward reform. In the news release of November 9, 1994, regarding the rejection of the Compton NewMedia patent application discussed in Chapter 3, the PTO said:

The PTO held public hearings Jan. 26–27 in San Jose, Calif., and Feb. 10–11 in Arlington, Va., on issues and problems surrounding the patenting of computer software-related inventions.

In response to the testimony gathered at the hearings, the PTO introduced legislation on Aug. 9 to reform the patent reexamination system by expanding the grounds upon which reexamination could be initiated, by allowing third parties greater participation in the proceedings and by providing third party participants an opportunity to appeal the outcome of the reexam.

On Sept. 30, the PTO also introduced legislation supporting the publication of patent applications 18 months after filing, a step the software industry has urged the PTO to take in order to make the agency's patent examination process more transparent. The legislation did not pass in the 103rd Congress, however, it will be reintroduced in the 104th Congress [in 1995–96].

Overall, I am optimistic about the future of intellectual property protection in the computer field. The courts are working hard, as is the PTO, to make the system work. One can only hope that everyone involved will cooperate with those efforts.

APPENDIXES

Appendix A:
A Review of the Fundamentals
of Computer Technology

THE COMPUTER

The history of copyright protection in the computer software area has consisted largely of finding the appropriate distinctions between copyright and patent protection.

Copyright protection, such as is commonly used for books and other writings, is well known and understood. Why is the computer so special in a discussion of copyright protection? Computer software, in particular, is quite different from a book. Although software is usually written on paper, when it is placed in the computer it causes that machine to do something. In that respect, it can appear to be more like part of a machine, and some have suggested that patent law would be more appropriate. To make sense out of all of this, we shall have to describe some of the characteristics of computers and how they work.

A computer is a problem-solving machine. It accepts and stores input in the form of instructions and data, it causes the data to be manipulated according to a sequence of instructions that it executes to solve the problem, and it produces output called the results. The set of possible instructions that a specific computer can perform is called its instruction set.

The solving of a problem on a computer starts with the input. What does input look like? It depends on whether one is interested in the medium, such as punched cards or paper, which carries the input information, or the information itself. It turns out that this apparently trivial distinction is extremely important when it comes to copyright protection. If a person originally writes instructions on a piece of paper, does putting those instructions into the computer change the nature of the information? Are the instructions now part of the computer? The argument has been made that once the instructions have been brought into the machine and are part of the computer, they are most appropriately covered by patent law, rather than copyright law. With that argument, the medium, and the role it plays in representing instructions and data, becomes part of the protection question.

Before we try to straighten out such issues, let us continue with our look at the computer itself. The physical part that we can see and touch is called the hardware. There is generally no question that hardware is most appropriately protected by patent law. But if we plug the physical computer into an electric outlet and turn it on, nothing will happen unless we cause it to execute some sequence of instructions. It is a kind of chicken-and-egg question as to how the computer can execute any instructions at all, when it needs instructions to do anything, such as obtaining the first instructions to be executed. The standard way this apparent paradox is resolved is to have a few appropriate instructions "wired in"; these constitute precisely the short sequence needed to bring in other instructions from some external device, such as a magnetic tape or disk. As soon as enough instructions are brought in in this way, they are the sequence of instructions next executed, and the computer is on its way. Not surprisingly, this set of events is called "bootstrapping."

The process, then, is to turn on the computer and press a button. This causes a few instructions (the initial program) to be executed. These instructions send signals to some external device, such as a magnetic disk where additional instructions are stored, to transmit a larger block of instructions to the computer and execute them. Once this has happened, the full capabilities of the computer are available.

In order to take a closer look at the format of instructions and the information contained there, we need to describe briefly the main components of a computer. We have already referred several times to external input devices. These take many forms, such as keyboards on terminals or personal computers, magnetic tape drives, magnetic (floppy or hard) disk drives, CD-ROMs, punched-paper-tape or punched-card readers, and even ordinary telephones with push-button tone-generating features. Any mechanism can qualify as an input device if it is capable of sending coded signals to the computer. We see such input devices showing up in great numbers now in automobiles, for example, where sensors take readings on the status of the carburetor or the brakes and send these data as input to computers that can regulate the fuel mixture or keep the automobile from skidding on ice. We will not be concerned here with the details of such input devices beyond their ability to send input data to the computer when requested, or when some special event occurs.

Corresponding to the input devices are the output devices, which convey results from the computer to the outside world for interpretation. Often these results are conveyed to a human, but with increasing frequency this output information is sent directly to another computer, for which it is, of course, input. Output devices include the familiar computer terminal with its presentation of information on a screen, the ubiquitous printer, and the disk drives and CD-ROMs mentioned earlier. The latter mechanisms serve as output devices when the computer is sending results to be written on them, and as input devices when the computer asks for information to be read back from them. The ordinary telephone, with a computer-generated synthetic spoken-voice sound, can also serve as an output device.

The result of all of the choices involved in selecting the hardware components and their capabilities, how to organize them, what operations the computer should be able to perform, and so on, is called the "architecture" of the computer. The architecture is usually described in written form. One way to think about it is that someone who understands the available hardware technologies should be able to build the computer from the architecture description. If two people independently built computers from the same architecture description, we might expect differences in the speed and the cost of the two machines, but not in their other problem-solving capabilities.

Where is information stored while it is being processed by the computer? Every computer has a component called "storage," or "memory," which retains information. This storage is almost always some kind of magnetic medium, in which the circuitry of the computer can distinguish two different states, for which we use the names zero and one. We will not be concerned with the actual physical characteristics of storage; it is sufficient for our purposes to visualize storage as an extremely long ribbon on which are temporarily painted a long string of zeros and ones:

000111110001010101011100000011101010101...001

We can certainly wonder how the computer finds anything in such a very long and apparently cryptic sequence of digits. The answer is that there is an implicit structure superimposed on the storage. There is a pattern to how information is represented there, and that pattern is the key to finding and interpreting that information.

To understand what is happening, we first look at how information is actually represented, or coded, in storage. The key question is how many different items need to be represented? To put it another way, how many different items of information must we be able to recognize, or distinguish from one another? The typical computer is designed to accommodate 256 different items, or characters. This allows us to include the 26 upper-case letters, the 26 lower-case letters, the 10 decimal digits, and a variety of special characters, such as +, -, *, (,), [,], {, }, ?, @, and many others. Still other characters are used to indicate when transmission of information between computers is to begin and end. It turns out that the number of characters needed for almost all of our usual purposes is somewhat less than 256, so we can conveniently accommodate the ones we need by allowing 256.[1] We shall soon see why that apparently strange choice of 256 turns out to be very convenient.

If we write all of the possible combinations of a pair of zeros and ones, we obtain

$$0\ 0$$
$$0\ 1$$
$$1\ 0$$
$$1\ 1$$

If we write the possible combinations for three digits, each of which can be zero or one, we obtain

$$0\ 0\ 0$$
$$0\ 0\ 1$$
$$0\ 1\ 0$$
$$0\ 1\ 1$$

$$1\ 0\ 0$$
$$1\ 0\ 1$$
$$1\ 1\ 0$$
$$1\ 1\ 1$$

We now see that adding another digit merely reproduces the entries in the previous group, once preceded by a zero, and once preceded by a one. In other words, adding another digit doubles the number of possibilities. Continuing in this way, we find that using four digits allows 16 entries, using seven digits yields 128 entries, and using eight digits provides for 256 entries in such a listing. Now all we need to do is assign one such entry to each character, and we can represent a sequence of characters by their corresponding sequences of zeros and ones.

Figure A.1 shows a portion of one common assignment of characters to zero-and-one patterns, called the USA Standard Code for Information Interchange (ASCII), adopted in 1968. The ASCII standard actually used seven-digit patterns, allowing 128 possible characters, but most computers have been designed around eight digits, allowing for future expansion to 256 different characters.

FIGURE A.1

A Portion of the ASCII 7-Bit Code

0100000	(space)
0100001	!
0100010	"
0100011	#
. . .	. . .
0101010	*
0101011	+
0101100	,
. . .	. . .
0110000	0
0110001	1
0110010	2
0110011	3
0110100	4
. . .	. . .
1000001	A
1000010	B
1000011	C
. . .	. . .
1001010	J
1001011	K
1001100	L
. . .	. . .
1100001	a
1100010	b
1100011	c
. . .	. . .
1101010	j
1101011	k
1101100	l
. . .	. . .
1110101	u
1110110	v
1110111	w
1111000	x
1111001	y
. . .	. . .

The eight-digit patterns used in most computers are called bytes, and the zeros and ones themselves, which can be viewed as binary choices, or binary digits, are usually referred to as bits. Thus, each byte contains eight bits. To illustrate the use of such assignments for characters, consider the string of characters "July 4, 1776." Using the ASCII seven-bit encoding shown in Figure A.1 for simplicity, the first seven characters of this string would be represented by the following sequence:

1001010	1110101	1101100	1111001	0100000	0110100	0101100
J	u	l	y	(space)	4	,

Note that even the space counts as a character, since otherwise there would be no way to know when printing these characters as output that a space was to be printed there. Since eight bits provide for 256 different characters, and most computers use this, we shall base the following discussion on eight-bit bytes.

Storage is normally organized into bytes, each consisting of eight bits; each byte represents a character in storage. In order to access this information, we associate with each byte position or location in storage its position number, or "address," starting with zero. Thus, the first byte location in storage is given the address 0, and the second one (beginning with the ninth bit) the address 1. If there were in some particular computer 50,000 bytes of storage, the addresses would range from 0 to 49,999. Looking ahead to our discussion of instructions, then, we might expect to see an instruction that, for example, could cause a particular number, say 3, to be placed in byte location 74, or an instruction that would move a copy of the contents of location 18 to location 92 (presumably replacing the previous contents of location 92).

A distinction is sometimes made between different types of storage. We have been referring to various locations in storage, how to name them in instructions, and how and when the values stored in them can be changed. This kind of storage is often called random-access memory (RAM) because any location can be accessed, and if needed, changed, in any sequence.[2] Another kind of storage is called read-only memory (ROM). Here one can also read values in various locations in any sequence, but values cannot be changed or written. They can only be read.

Another component of a typical computer is the Central Processing Unit (CPU). This is where the action is. There are generally two main parts to the CPU. The most visible part is the Arithmetic/Logic Unit (ALU). This unit usually consists of a number of registers, each capable of temporarily holding one or more bytes. The contents of these registers are involved in arithmetic computation, such as adding numbers, and also in logical decisions, such as testing for positive or negative numbers, in order to decide which of several possible courses of action to undertake next. The registers are generally numbered, so we have Register 0, Register 1, and so on, up to perhaps Register 255. To go with such registers we usually have a variety of instructions, such as an instruction to load the contents of storage location 1352 into Register 3, or add the contents of location 2345 to the contents of Register 4 and store the results into Register 12.

The other main component of the CPU is the Control Unit. The activities of the Control Unit are generally hidden from anyone using the computer. Its role is to coordinate the actions of all of the other parts of the system so they occur at just the right moment and have precisely the desired effect. In addition, after the execution of each instruction, the Control Unit is responsible for determining which is the next instruction that should be executed.

Usually, the next instruction is the one located sequentially in the next location in storage (remembering that instructions are retained in storage just like data). On some occasions an instruction involves making a decision. For example, there might be a test to determine whether the contents of some register in the ALU are negative. The effect of an affirmative response to that question may be not to select the next sequentially located instruction for execution, but some other instruction instead. Once the instruction containing the test is executed, its successor will be selected based on the result of the test, and the computer will be off on a possibly different sequence of instructions from its previous path. It is analogous to making the decision to turn right at some corner while driving in a city. The car that makes that turn is now on a very different route from another car that did not make that turn, although the basic decision apparently only affected the traversal of a particular intersection. It is through the use of such logical decisions that very complex computational sequences can be created to solve difficult and complicated problems.

SOFTWARE

Now it is time to take a closer look at the instructions that make up a computer program. The trend throughout the recent history of programming has been to provide easier-to-use languages with which to communicate instructions to the computer. A person with only a limited acquaintance with programming can instruct a computer with such statements as

```
{Begin computation}
  Year := IYear;
  while (Year <= LYear) and (Bal > 0.0) do begin
    if (Year = LYear) then
      LastMonth := LMonth
    else
      LastMonth := 12;
    writeln(Year);
```

This is part of a program shown in Figure A.4. In the early days (that is, the 1950s), such languages were not available, and programming was done at the level of very primitive details about the structure and organization of the computer itself, instead of being concerned more with the problem being solved. We shall develop some of the ideas leading to such higher-level languages, as they are called.

What do we usually want to accomplish with an instruction? In the simplest case, we want to perform an operation on some data. Therefore the instruction must contain the operation we want the computer to do, such as addition or subtraction; what data we want to do it to (or at least where to find it); where we should put the result; and anything unusual about the selection of the next instruction to be executed. In fact, a typical instruction might have the structure:

What to do	What to do it to	Where to put the result	Where to find the next instruction

In many computers one or more of these parts (called fields) is often omitted. Omitting a field implies that it should have some standard value. Let us look at these four parts of an instruction.

What Operation To Do

One of the first things the designer of a new computer must determine, or specify, is the set of actions or operations the computer is expected to carry out. These will no doubt always include add and subtract. Surprisingly, some computers have in the past been designed without including specific provisions for doing multiplication and division, because multiplication can be accomplished by repeated additions, and division by repeated subtractions. Multiplication and division require somewhat complicated circuitry, so it is not altogether surprising that in some cases the designer might opt for simplicity (with resulting lower costs), and put a little more burden on the programmer. The person writing the program of instructions must then achieve the multiplication result by requesting repeated additions. Although this inevitably causes the computer to run somewhat slower, because it must find, interpret, and carry out more instructions, it has been done on some machines.[3]

Typically, a sequence of arithmetic operations in a program will leave some result in a particular place, either in a selected register in the ALU or a designated location in storage, and there will then be an instruction that will examine the contents of that location or register and cause a decision to be made as to the selection of the next instruction to be executed, as we have already discussed.

For example, a sequence of instructions might examine an account number that was supplied as input to the program. If it is a valid account number, 0 would be put into Register 7, otherwise, the value 1 would be put there. Then a subsequent instruction would test Register 7. If it found a 1 there, a "jump" would be made to an error-reporting sequence of instructions; otherwise, the program execution would continue as if nothing had happened.

There will be other kinds of operations to be performed as well, such as initiating some input or output, causing some musical sound to be generated, or causing a bell to ring. We need not go into much detail here, except to recognize that a fairly large number of different operation designations, or codes, must be available and recognizable by the Control Unit. To provide for about 200 operation codes, we might specify that each instruction should include eight bits — one full byte — to indicate which operation is to be performed. As we have already seen, eight bits allows 256 distinct operation codes, so we could actually accommodate our 200 desired operations and allow for 56 others to be assigned in the future. That is in fact what is usually done; the designer allows for additional codes to be assigned later, once the computer is on the market and in use. Only then is it possible to see how the customers create patterns of use for that computer. If it becomes clear that some particular popular operation, such as multiplication, really should have been there in the first place, it could be added.

What Data To Do It To

It sometimes happens that we know that we want to add a particular number to some other number. We might also want to add two values that will be different every time we have a particular problem to solve. For example, in a payroll program, it will often be the case that we will know that we want to add this week's hours worked to the total hours worked so far this month, to obtain the new total hours worked. If we are going to write the instructions to do that, however, we really do not know the actual values to use until we run the payroll, and those values will change from person to person. In writing the instructions, therefore, we can only instruct the computer to go to the locations where Current-Hours-Worked and Total-Hours-Worked will be stored, and to use whatever values are found there. That way, the same instructions could work not only for each time period, but for every employee.

An instruction must always indicate where the data is to be found. The data may be either in a register in the ALU as a result of a previous instruction or it may be in a location in storage. Each instruction therefore designates the location of the data on which the instruction is to act. On the other hand, on some computers we find instructions that include specific small, often-used constants right in the instruction. As an example of this, some computers include a built-in instruction to add to, or increment, a register by a small number, in fact, any number between 0 and 255. This instruction might take the form:

inc   3, 5

which would mean; "Increment Register 3 by the value 5." Putting the constant 5 directly into the instruction saves creating it in a storage location and then obtaining it when that particular action was to take place.

Every time we shall make a general statement about computers, such as how instructions are written, there will be a small number of computers that do not conform to that description. Those exceptions are to be expected when there are so many choices to be made in how computers can be designed and programmed. In fact, that is one way in which new inventions are created. New combinations of choices are made that have not been made before, and a new method, or a new process, is invented.

Where To Put the Result

One of the most common outcomes of a computation is a new result that must be saved, such as the newly updated Total-Hours-Worked. It may be that this new value is to replace the old value, but it might also be true that for the next instruction about to be executed both the old and the new values are needed, and only at the end will the new value be stored on top of, and thus wipe out, the old value. We must be able, therefore, to specify where the result of each computation is to be stored, however temporarily. For this reason, the format of the instruction typically includes a result field, either an ALU register number or the address of a storage location, which is used to indicate where the result of the operation is to be put.

Where To Find the Next Instruction

The fourth field in the typical format instruction we have been considering indicates where in storage the next instruction should be found. However, this field is often omitted in the design of the instruction format, as we will see below.

THE FORMAT OF AN INSTRUCTION

Given that an instruction must include the four components that we have described, and that the control unit must be able to analyze every instruction to find those components, it is clear that each instruction must conform to a standard format, or structure. For example, in a particular computer an instruction might consist of 36 bits, allocated as follows:

operation	register	result location	next instruction location
11110010	0011	000011101010	111000101010

where all the bits would be physically next to each other in storage, but where we have spaced them here to illustrate their intended interpretations. The first group, or field, represents the operation code (with the 8 bits allowing 256 possible codes for this purpose). The second field shows the number of a register in the ALU containing the data on which this particular operation will be carried out (with 4 bits allowing reference to 16 registers in this example). The third field provides the address of the location in storage where the result is to be placed after the computation (in this case the binary representation of the decimal number 234), and the fourth field indicates the location of the next instruction.

Every computer has its own format for instructions, and many have several formats for different kinds of actions to be taken. Sometimes there is no field for the next instruction location. In such cases, it is always understood to be the next instruction in storage after the current one, unless the operation code indicates otherwise.[4] We shall not be concerned with further details of instruction formats. Suffice it to say that anyone who wants to produce instructions in the form of zeros and ones for a particular machine must be familiar with the formats for that machine.

The normal reaction to the last sentence of the preceding paragraph is no doubt a slight bit of incredulity. Who in his right mind would want to produce instructions for a computer in the form of strings of zeros and ones? You may be sure that this was also the reaction of the computer pioneers in the late 1940s and early 1950s. They very quickly began writing instructions in the form of alphabetic codes and symbols, such as:

read	a,b,c
load	3,a
add	3,b
sub	3,c
store	3,x
print	a,b,c,x

where the intent of this sequence is to read three values into storage locations to be referred to as a, b, and c, then load the value in location a into Register 3 of the ALU, then add the value in location b to the value in Register 3, subtract the value in location c from the value in Register 3, store the result in a storage location called x, and finally print the values in locations a, b, c, and x.

In the good old days, the person writing this would then laboriously translate each instruction manually into the corresponding zeros and ones before entering them into the computer for execution. This process consisted of looking up the binary code for add, the code for store, and so on, picking specific storage addresses for a, b, c, and x, and then writing it all out in binary form, in zeros and ones, a very tedious and error-prone activity.[5]

This state of affairs did not last very long, fortunately, because someone soon realized that the manual translation that the programmer was doing could be done by a computer instead. After all, writing the instructions was the creative part. The rest was a routine clerical task, which was precisely what the computer was invented for. The last program that was manually translated was probably the program that from then on did that translation. This translation program is usually called an "assembler," because it assembles instructions.

The creativity did not stop there. What that last example really wanted to accomplish was to bring in as input the values for a, b, and c, compute

$$x = a + b - c$$

and print the new values of a, b, c, and x. What the author really wanted to write as a program, then, was something like the following:

```
read a, b, c
compute x = a + b - c
print a, b, c, x
```

or maybe even

```
read (a, b, c) and print (a, b, c, and x = a + b - c)
```

We refer to these more abstract versions (relative to the detailed zeros and ones, or even to the assembler language), as written in a high-level language. It is easy to see why programs are now written in such high-level languages whenever possible, although for many years quite complex programs and even whole systems were written in the symbolic assembler language.

TRANSLATORS

Having discussed at some length how computers can only "understand" zeros and ones, we are now faced with the problem of converting such statements as

```
read (a, b, c) and print (a, b, c, and x = a + b - c)
```

into zeros and ones. We indicated earlier that when the notation of the assembler language, such as

```
read      a,b,c
load      3,a
add       3,b
```

was developed, people had to manually translate that notation into the zeros and ones. The resulting code was called the object code for historical reasons, probably because it was the object of the whole exercise.

It was harder to take much more complex statements, such as

read (a, b, c) and print (a, b, c, and x = a + b - c)

and figure out what object code was needed to carry out the corresponding computation. On average, about ten assembler-level instructions are needed for each such high-level language statement. Consider that ten is an average; simple statements like:

set x = y

generate only two simple instructions:

```
load      1,y
store     1,x
```

(using Register 1 in the ALU this time), while some high-level statements generate many more than ten. Figuring out which instructions to generate to be the object-code equivalent of perhaps thousands of statements in a complex program is not an easy task. While assemblers appeared in 1950, very early in the life of the computer industry,[6] it took until 1956 for FORTRAN (Formula Translator), generally considered the first successful high-level language translator, to appear. Currently there are many such languages, and an important segment of the software industry is engaged in creating and marketing translators, called compilers, for various high-level languages to run on a wide variety of computers.

Why are there a large number of high-level languages? It would seem that once such a language was developed, assuming it was indeed fairly general, you could write just about whatever program was needed. Given the creative nature of computer programmers, however, it is not surprising that as soon as one language appeared, someone else had a better idea as to how to express the computation to be done. This was especially true if the language was intended to be used for a particular class of problems, such as business-oriented problems or scientific problems. Over the years, special languages appeared for specifying the actions of numerically controlled milling machines, for solving particular kinds of mathematical equations, and for solving problems using artificial intelligence techniques. Sammet (1969) contains descriptions of about 200 such languages. Since then, other languages have appeared, while earlier ones have fallen into disuse. From time to time, some attempts have been made to standardize on a language that everyone could use, but for the reasons given, no clear single standard has evolved. A few languages, such as FORTRAN, COBOL, PL/1, BASIC, Pascal, C, C++, Ada, LISP, and a few others, are now much more widely used than the rest, and standard versions of many of these have been agreed upon, but a number of different languages are used in the industry.

Each of these higher-level languages in which programs are written must have a translator to convert statements from that high-level language into object code, the zeros and ones. Let us take a quick look at how a translator might do its job. First, let us look at an example of a relatively small high-level language program. Figure A.2 is a FORTRAN program that I have been using for many years to compute and print the amortization table of a loan, given the initial balance of the loan, the interest rate, the amount of the monthly payment, and the starting and ending months and years. It is not necessary that you understand this program, only that you follow the general flow, and that you believe that following these specific instructions will solve the problem at hand. The lines starting with "C" are comments that do not initiate any action; they help the human reader understand what is going on.[7]

FIGURE A.2
A FORTRAN Program for Amortization

```
C       ASK FOR INPUT DATA
1               WRITE(0,600)
600             FORMAT('1ENTER BALANCE, RATE, STARTING MONTH, ',
        X       'YEAR, ENDING MONTH, YEAR, MONTHLY PAYMENT')
                READ(5,700) BAL,RATE,IM,IYEAR,LM,LYEAR,XPAY
700             FORMAT(F9.2,F5.3,2(I3,I5),F7.2)

C       INITIALIZE VARIABLES
                SINT=0.0
                RRATE=RATE*100.
```

Figure A.2, continued

```
C          PRINT HEADINGS ON OUTPUT
           WRITE(6,100)BAL,RRATE
100        FORMAT('1INITIAL BALANCE = $', F12.2,20X,
         X 'INTEREST RATE =',F8.3,'%')
           WRITE(6,200)
200        FORMAT('0',20X,'MONTH',10X,'PAYMENT',10X,'INTEREST',
         X 10X,'PRINCIPAL',10X,'NEW BALANCE')

C          BEGIN THE COMPUTATION
           DO 10 IY=IYEAR,3000
           WRITE(6,300)IY
300        FORMAT('0',I10)
           YINT = 0.0
           DO 9 M=IM,12
20         XI=(RATE/12.0)*BAL

C          ROUND INTEREST VALUE TO TWO PLACES
           IRDD = (XI*1000. + 5.) / 10.
           XI = IRDD / 100.
           XPRT=XPAY-XI

C          ROUND PRINCIPAL PAYMENT
           IRDD = (XPRT * 1000. + 5.) / 10.
           XPRT = IRDD / 100.

C          COMPUTE BALANCE WITH APPROPRIATE ROUNDING
           ISAVE=BAL/10000.
           X1=BAL-ISAVE*10000.
           IRDD = (X1 * 1000. + 5.) / 10.
           X1 = IRDD / 100.
           X2=X1-XPRT
           IRDD = (X2 * 1000. + 5.) / 10.
           BAL = IRDD / 100.+ISAVE*10000.
           SINT=SINT+XI
           YINT = YINT + XI
           IF (BAL .GE. 0) GO TO 30
           XPAY = XPAY + BAL
           XPRT = XPRT + BAL
           BAL = 0.0
30         WRITE(6,400)M,XPAY,XI,XPRT,BAL
400        FORMAT(I25,F18.2,F16.2,F20.2,F21.2)

C          ARE WE DONE YET?
           IF (BAL .LE. 0 .OR. M .EQ. LM .AND. LYEAR .EQ. IY) GO TO 11
9          CONTINUE
```

```
            WRITE(6,800) YINT
800         FORMAT('0INTEREST THIS YEAR = $',F10.2)
10          IM=1
11          WRITE(6,800) YINT
            WRITE(6,500)SINT
500         FORMAT('0TOTAL INTEREST PAID = $',F10.2)
            GO TO 1
            END
```

The final computed output of this program for a small loan is shown in Figure A.3. The input values, that is, the values entered by the user in response to requests from the program that were used to produce Figure A.3, were for a loan of $500, an interest rate of 7 percent, and monthly payments of $50, to start in April 1992 and continue until the loan would be paid.

FIGURE A.3
The Output of the Amortization Program

INITIAL BALANCE = $500.00
INTEREST RATE = 7.000%

	MONTH	PAYMENT	INTEREST	PRINCIPAL	NEW BALANCE
1992	4	50.00	2.92	47.08	452.92
	5	50.00	2.64	47.36	405.56
	6	50.00	2.37	47.63	357.93
	7	50.00	2.09	47.91	310.02
	8	50.00	1.81	48.19	261.83
	9	50.00	1.53	48.47	213.36
	10	50.00	1.24	48.76	164.60
	11	50.00	0.96	49.04	115.56
	12	50.00	0.67	49.33	66.23

INTEREST THIS YEAR = $16.23

	MONTH	PAYMENT	INTEREST	PRINCIPAL	NEW BALANCE
1993	1	50.00	0.39	49.61	16.62
	2	16.72	0.10	16.62	0.00

INTEREST THIS YEAR = $0.49
TOTAL INTEREST PAID = $16.72

What would the FORTRAN translator do with the program in Figure A.2? It would read one line of the program at a time, digest it, that is, identify the separate words, numbers, and special punctuation marks, "understand" what the author had in mind, and generate corresponding primitive machine-language instructions to carry out the actions of the individual statements. Not all high-level statements cause primitive instructions to be generated. Some statements, those with an initial "C," are merely comments to indicate to the human reader some information about the computation that follows. Another statement that does not generate primitive instructions is the statement labelled 600 in Figure A.2, which indicates which format to use to print the request to the person to enter some input values. However, most statements do generate primitive instructions, such as the two statements that compute SINT and RRATE immediately after the statement labelled 700.

The important thing to remember is that the FORTRAN translator reads as its input for its own computation (that is, the translation process) the FORTRAN program written in the form of more or less English statements, and it generates a machine-language version of the program, full of zeros and ones, which no human would want to read. The machine-language version, the object code, is the same program in a different language. When the translation process is finished and the object code has been generated and storage arranged for values of the variables, then the actual computation to compute the amortization of a loan can begin. When the object code itself is executed, the program will do all of the things the author intended. It will ask for input values, compute all of the balances and interest payments, and print the output. Note that the object program can be saved and run a number of times without going through the translation process again.

A useful analogy to keep in mind, when we look at these events from the point of view of copyright protection, is to consider what happens at the United Nations when an important speech is about to be delivered. The speaker will probably distribute the text of the speech to the press ahead of time, presumably with permission to publish it. The foreign correspondents will immediately translate the speech into their own languages so they can excerpt parts of it for their own media as soon as the speech is given, if not before. The translated versions of the speech are still the same speech, but in a different language. At that point, the speech itself has not yet been given. In copyright terms, the translated version is a derivative work.

There is another concept, interpretation, that will be needed later, and that is easily distinguished from translation in terms of the United

Nations example. If someone does not need a translated version on paper but wants to listen to the speech as it is given, there are usually interpreters available who will listen to each sentence as it is spoken, and provide the interpretation in another language. At the end of the speech there is no translated version, but each sentence was understood by the listener as the speech was given.

Looking ahead to some of the problems with the copyright law when it is applied to software, suppose someone wants a version of a copyrighted program to run on a different computer from the one for which it was written, but the other computer does not have a translator for the language in which the program was written. That means that the programmer must rewrite the program in another language for which a translator does exist on the target computer. Because the target computer has different characteristics that inevitably affect even high-level language versions of programs, is the resulting program, written in a different language for a different computer, the same program? Is it close enough to call making such a new copy without permission a violation of the Copyright Act? What are the guidelines according to which a decision can be made? Suppose the writer changes many, or all, of the names of variables, the formats of input requests and of the printed output, and other details of the visual characteristics of the program? How much must be changed to be able to call the result "different," or "not substantially similar"?

Take a case that is perhaps simpler. Figure A.4 shows the FORTRAN amortization program rewritten in the Pascal language. (Here comments are enclosed in braces: { }.) The two programs look quite different, but even a cursory analysis shows that the same logic was used, pretty much the same order of events, and so on. Is creating this version a copyright infringement if no permission was given to do it?

FIGURE A.4
The Amortization Program in Pascal

```
program Amortization (input, output);
  var
    Bal, Rate, Payment, SumInt, RealRate, Int, PrincPay : real;
    IRounded, YInt, ISave, Temp1, Temp2 : real;
    IMonth, IYear, LMonth, LYear, Year, Month, LastMonth : integer;
  begin
    {Ask for input data}
    writeln('Enter Balance, Rate, Starting Month and Year, ',
        'Ending Month and Year, and Monthly Payment');
    readln(Bal, Rate, IMonth, IYear, LMonth, LYear, Payment);
```

Figure A.4, continued

```
{Initialize variables}
SumInt := 0.0;
RealRate := Rate * 100.0;

{Print headings on output}
writeln('Initial Balance = $', Bal : 8 : 2, '  Interest Rate = ', RealRate : 4 : 2,
    '%');
  writeln('  Month', '    Payment', '  Interest',   'Principal', '  New Balance');

{Begin the computation}
  Year := IYear;
  while (Year <= LYear) and (Bal > 0.0) do
      begin
    if (Year = LYear) then
      LastMonth := LMonth
    else
      LastMonth := 12;
    writeln(Year);
    YInt := 0.0;
    Month := IMonth;
    while (Month <= LastMonth) and (Bal > 0.0) do
      begin
        Int := (Rate / 12.0) * Bal;

      {Round interest value to two places}
        IRounded := (Int * 1000.0 + 5.0) / 10.0;
        Int := IRounded / 100.0;
        PrincPay := Payment - Int;

      {Round Principal Payment}
        IRounded := (PrincPay * 1000.0 + 5.0) / 10.0;
        PrincPay := IRounded / 100.0;

      {Compute Balance with Appropriate Rounding}
        ISave := Bal / 10000.0;
        Temp1 := Bal - ISave * 10000.0;
        IRounded := (Temp1 * 1000.0 + 5.0) / 10.0;
        Temp1 := IRounded / 100.0;
        Temp2 := Temp1 - PrincPay;
        IRounded := (Temp2 * 1000.0 + 5.0) / 10.0;
        Bal := IRounded / 100.0 + ISave * 10000.0;
        SumInt := SumInt + Int;
        YInt := YInt + Int;
```

```
        if Bal < 0.0 then
            begin
                Payment := Payment + Bal;
                PrincPay := PrincPay + Bal;
                Bal := 0.0
            end;
            writeln(Month : 9, Payment : 13 : 2, Int : 11 : 2,
                PrincPay : 12 : 2, Bal : 14 : 2);
            Month := Month + 1;
        end;
        writeln;
        writeln('Interest this year = $', YInt : 6 : 2);
        Year := Year + 1
    end;
    writeln;

    {Are we done yet?}
    writeln('Total Interest Paid = $', SumInt : 6 : 2)
end.
```

OPERATING SYSTEMS

We have now seen what a real program looks like. Typically the program contains some declarations and comments, some statements to call for input, a number of computation statements, and then output statements to communicate the results. More complicated programs also contain calls to pre-packaged programs in libraries to carry out special kinds of computation that occur fairly often, such as sorting tables of information, computing complex mathematical functions, preparing an index for a book, generating a real-estate form for a common type of mortgage, displaying a standard background on a screen, and so on. Because such applications of computers occur frequently and almost all uses of these programs are essentially the same, we can prepare generic versions, put them into a library, and use them as needed.

We have already seen instances of the use of such library programs in the FORTRAN and Pascal amortization examples. To call for input the Pascal program in Figure A.4 called upon readln (pronounced "read line"), a utility program for reading input one line at a time. Similarly, when the program was ready to write a line to the output device, either the printer or the user's screen, there was a call to writeln (pronounced "write line"). The information in parentheses after the name of the program being called informs that program about the specifics of that particular call. Thus, in the last occurrence of a call on writeln, two items are to be printed on a line, the character string "Total Interest Paid = $" and the value of the variable SumInt, which accumulates the total interest paid. There are also indications that the latter value is to appear in a space six characters wide, with two digits following the decimal point.

As a further example, suppose we anticipated that we would frequently need to call on a loan amortization program. Certainly a programmer designing a software system for a Savings & Loan office would want to arrange to have such a program readily available. The programmer might take the program we wrote earlier and make it even more general, perhaps by allowing the payments to be made quarterly instead of monthly, if the customer requested it. The program might also contain a provision for specifying the total number of periods in which payments were to be made, and letting the program determine the size of the payment needed to come out even at the end. Once the program was fully specified, designed, coded, and debugged, it would be placed in the library of programs so that it could be called by other programs. Appropriate documentation would then be written to tell anyone authorized to use it just how to write the call for the library program into a calling program. This would include directions on how to convey to the program the specific amounts and rates needed as input, and the choices among the various options, such as whether payments were to be made monthly or quarterly, and so on. One advantage of such increased generality is that the same program could be called several times during the solution of one problem, so the person applying for a mortgage could try different kinds of loans to see which would be best under his or her particular circumstances. A loan office providing such services might have an advantage over one that could not so easily provide such information.

A library of packaged programs, often called subroutines or utility programs, is only one of many components of the typical operating system on a computer. The operating system is software usually provided or sold by the vendor of the hardware. Its role is to coordinate the uses of the various software components that are available to serve the user and make it easier to use the computer system. The operating system determines the order in which user application programs will be executed, which resources such as storage space, disk facilities, and execution time will be allocated to each program, and how much different users of a system will be charged.

To elaborate, imagine a large system serving perhaps hundreds of users simultaneously, such as an airline reservation system. Each person wants an immediate response from the system, as if it were only working for him or her. To accomplish this very quick response to each user, the system must service each person rapidly for an extremely short time. This so-called time slice is actually measured in milliseconds, that is, thousandths of a second, and such a system is called a time-sharing system. No one user has the information or the incentive to arrange to use only a few milliseconds of time and then hand the computer over to someone else for a turn. Moreover, no one user has the information or the motivation to use only a portion of the available storage so someone else can use a different part of it during the next time slice. There has to be a global coordinator with total information about all user programs currently running so time, storage, and other resources can be partitioned equitably among them. In addition, if there is to be a fair charging mechanism for using resources, there has to be a global accounting system that determines which resources are being used by each application program, measured in terms of milliseconds, if not microseconds (millionths of a second).

Another feature of operating systems is the provision of translators for programs written in high-level languages. When a program is written, say in Pascal such as in Figure A.4, the Pascal translator must be called upon to translate the program into the object code version so it can be executed. Operating systems often provide in their libraries translators for dozens of popular languages, ready to be called upon whenever a source program is introduced that needs translation. There is still some debate as to whether such translators should be considered part of the operating system or regarded as application programs. The distinction between operating systems and application programs has been an issue in at least one major copyright case, *Apple Computer Inc.* v. *Formula International, Inc.*, which was introduced in Chapter 4.

Although we have characterized a common form of operating system as serving a number of users simultaneously in a general time-sharing system, there are also a number of operating systems in use in personal, one-person workstations. These operating systems do not have to allocate resources among many users, and they do not have to do the usual accounting to charge different users for the resources they use. However, these operating systems do provide a great many services, even to a single user. They include a complete library of utility programs, and they provide input and output services. They also keep track of the files or documents that the user creates. In some systems the files are organized with directories and subdirectories maintained by the operating system. In other systems the user creates documents and stores them in folders, which may contain other folders. In these cases, the user depends on the operating system to keep track of the files or documents, and the hierarchical relationships among them. Other services include copying files or documents to and from disks, duplicating files or documents, user-interface management, and other housekeeping tasks. The operating system for a single user on a personal workstation may be simpler than the general time-sharing system found on larger computers, but it is sophisticated and complex software.

The general flow of activity when someone needs to solve a problem can now be summarized, tying together a number of concepts that have been explained up to this point. Once a problem and its requirements have been identified, the algorithm needed to solve it is designed, and a high-level language is selected. The application program is then written in the high-level language, keyed, or scanned into the computer and stored, usually on a disk, to await translation. Eventually the translator for that language is called and executed. Its input is the application program. The result of the translation, the object code, is generated and is usually also stored on the disk for future execution. When the object code is to be executed, it is brought into primary storage, and the object code versions of the various utility or library programs that it will call during execution are also brought in from the operating system library. Once all of the object code for all these programs is in place and properly linked together, execution can begin.

The starting point of the user's application program determines the first instruction to be executed, and the flow of instructions follows the usual rule by which subsequent instructions are selected, with branching to other parts of the program caused by decisions in the program. Occasionally the application program will call on one of the utility programs. That program will execute, and the application program will take over again. Eventually the problem will be solved, and the program's execution will end. At that point, the operating system will immediately select another user's application program, if there is one waiting, and the entire process just described will begin again. Actually, as we indicated earlier, because perhaps hundreds of users may be expecting such services at the same time, all of the steps outlined above will be occurring for all of them, a few milliseconds for each in turn, so quickly that each will not know the others are there.

If the steps in the preceding paragraphs are analyzed in detail, it will be clear that there is some very complex software causing a great variety of actions to take place, involving the very rapid movement of information between secondary storage (the disks) and primary storage, the sequencing of programs as to which execute at which times, and so on. All of this is hidden from the user, but it is clearly software. Some of the key copyright infringement cases have revolved around the protection of operating systems. Because they are so hidden from the user of the system, it has been argued that the operating system is part of the computer, hence equivalent to hardware. Another argument used in litigation defense against copyright infringement claims is that it does no more than make it possible to use the hardware in a routine way and hence is not copyrightable.

The important point to remember is that an operating system is software that consists of many programs. What has complicated the situation in some cases is that for efficiency reasons, some aspects of some operating systems have in fact been embedded into the hardware, causing the boundary between hardware and software to become somewhat fuzzy. This boundary is quite important in legal matters because hardware is not protectable by copyright, although computer architects have begun to move functionality back and forth between hardware and software for reasons that have nothing to do with intellectual property protection.

THE USER INTERFACE

We have all heard about user-friendly computers. What does the term mean? What does it have to do with copyright protection? It is important to understand how the underlying computer concepts are involved in making a computer program user-friendly.

In the example of Figure A.4, the amortization program, we saw that input was requested from the user of the program by displaying input requests, or prompts:

```
writeln('Enter Balance, Rate, Starting Month and Year, ',
    'Ending Month and Year, and Monthly Payment');
readln(Bal, Rate, IMonth, IYear, LMonth, LYear, Payment);
```

Here the programmer arranged for the prompt

Enter Balance, Rate, Starting Month and Year, Ending Month and Year, and Monthly Payment

to appear on the screen,[8] to remind the user which values to supply to the program, and in which order. In the earlier FORTRAN version, we saw a similar prompt, using the more detailed FORTRAN format statement:

```
1          WRITE(0,600)
600        FORMAT('1ENTER BALANCE, RATE, STARTING MONTH, ',
       X   'YEAR, ENDING MONTH, YEAR, MONTHLY PAYMENT')
           READ(5,700) BAL,RATE,IM,IYEAR,LM,LYEAR,XPAY
700        FORMAT(F9.2,F5.3,2(I3,I5),F7.2)
```

which would present the following prompt:[9]

**ENTER BALANCE, RATE, STARTING MONTH, YEAR, ENDING MONTH,
YEAR, MONTHLY PAYMENT**

The programmer was probably assuming here that the user would not necessarily be using the program constantly, and would appreciate a reminder of the order in which the data values should be entered. Of course, in that small example it was not very important to make the user interface more elaborate than a list of values to be entered at the keyboard. On the other hand, if that program were marketed to compete with others, the programmer would most likely spend a considerable amount of time designing the user interface so it would be pleasing to the eye, and it might even make full use of color. It would check for reasonable input values, such as an annual interest rate between 1 percent and 20 percent and starting and ending months between 1 and 12, and so on. In fact, one could decide to accept month names as an alternative to month numbers. It is easy to see that many choices are available, if the programmer wants to make the user interface friendly and easy to use.

Another set of choices available to the programmer, depending on the assumed capabilities of the user's workstation, is in the presentation of the prompts on the screen. The program fragments shown above are really oriented toward input devices that display one line at a time on a screen or typewriter-like device and accept one line at a time from a keyboard. Given the availability of a two-dimensional presentation on a screen, we could choose the location of the prompts on the screen and allow the user to enter the values in appropriate positions on the screen in any order. We might then ask only that a signal be given when all of the values have been entered. This might be a click of the mouse button when the cursor is in a certain location on the screen, or the depression of a particular key on the keyboard. In fact, if we really want to be friendly, we can make the program recognize the particular user for whom the program is running, recall the values that that person used the last time the program was run, and present those values on the screen as part of the prompt. Then the user need change only those values that are different this time. Perhaps even more useful would be to remember the entire history of this user's executions of this program, perform a statistical analysis of the values used, and present as the starting set of values the most likely values, based on the entire history. Perhaps that is going too far, but perhaps not, given the competitive nature of the software market.

Taking all of these ideas into account, the programmer might develop a program that would generate a display screen like the following, probably with the addition of color to highlight the value that the user is considering changing:

Amortization Program

Balance: $30,000.00	Annual Interest Rate: 7%
Starting Month and Year:	April, 1989
Ending Month and Year:	April, 2009
Monthly Payment:	$150.00

Press "Return" to calculate the loan schedule

Clearly, this is not the only way to ask for this information. In this case the programmer followed the order in which the original program asked for the input values. Someone else might find it much more natural, in working on a loan, to enter the size of the monthly payment immediately after indicating the amount of the loan. Should the amount of the loan be called "Amount of Loan," instead of "Balance"?

In this example, the programmer included the copyright marker at the bottom of the screen. Recent changes in the regulations covering copyright protection have made it no longer necessary to put the marker explicitly on the material to be protected. This programmer clearly wanted everyone who used the program to know that My Software, Inc. intended to protect that copyright diligently. What kind of protection was the company hoping to obtain in this way? Was it intended to cover the software, that is, the computer program that generated the image on the screen? Was it protecting the image on the screen itself? Both? If the company intended to protect the image on the screen, how much latitude would a competitor have in designing a similar but different screen presentation for the same kind of program? How different would it have to be to not be an infringement of the copyright thus claimed by My Software, Inc. if done without permission?

Let us return for a moment to the program needed to generate the screen we have just seen. How would the program check, for example, that the annual interest rate would be between 1 percent and 20 percent? How would the program prevent the user from changing the words Annual Interest Rate to something else? The answer is that the utility programs that are usually available in the operating system library for generating graphics on screens normally provide for displaying text or other graphics on the screen in protected areas, which the user of the program cannot change. The only parts of the screen that are subject to change are those that the programmer makes available to the user, such as the places where there are values that the user is in fact invited to modify. Once those values are in place, and the user signals that all changes have been made, the program can determine which values have changed. Each such value can then be tested against reasonable limits, as we have discussed earlier, such as the annual interest rate being between 1 percent and 20 percent, and the user can be prompted for correct values in case a mistake was made. It is very easy to hit an extra key and enter the value 89 percent, for example, instead of 8 percent, and thus make the computation meaningless.

In this discussion we have been concerned primarily with the content of the information presented to the user of a program. Modern workstations and personal computers are not restricted to lines containing characters, such as we have illustrated in the example here. The screens used today can put a different color or shade of color at every point on the screen (called a "pixel"). As a result, elaborate graphical user-interface-generating programs have become available, so every application programmer can create extremely friendly screen presentations. Many of us are now accustomed to the desktop metaphor, in which the illusion is created of working with pieces of paper on a desktop. The very similarity of some of these graphical user interfaces has led to significant litigation, as in *Lotus* v. *Paperback* and *Apple Computer, Inc.* v. *Microsoft, Inc.*

Given all of the kinds of choices that are available in designing the user interface, the issues with regard to copyright have to do with what aspects of the program and screen presentation can in fact be protected, how different a competitor's version can or must be to avoid charges of infringement, and how one would argue infringement in any case.

MACROS, PARAMETERS, AND MICROCODE

To complete our review of the hardware and software, we consider three somewhat technical issues that have appeared in recent intellectual property litigation: macros, parameter lists, and microcode. Here we shall review the technical aspects of these issues; their role in litigation will be considered in the context of the litigation.

Macros

The term "macro" is a shortened form of "macro-instruction." The idea is to create a new kind of instruction for the computer that is in some sense much larger than a normal instruction. In practice, it amounts to creating a kind of short-hand notation for commonly used sequences of ordinary instructions, so a person writing a program will not have to write out long sequences of very similar instructions over and over again. Macros, therefore, play the role of jargon in speech.

In ordinary communication, we use jargon, or abbreviations, so that we can say or write a very short sequence of sounds or symbols, and the listener or reader will supply the appropriate context and interpretation needed to understand what is meant. In programming, macros are usually created by a programmer for his or her own use. Sometimes a group of programmers will agree on a common set of macros and put them into a library for their joint use, but a different set of programmers working independently would probably have a different collection of macros, representing their choice of short-hand notations.

An example of such a concept outside the computer field, although probably implemented by a computer in any case, can be found on a home Video Cassette Recorder, or VCR/TV, system. A typical system provides a menu of commands on the screen of the TV set; the commands can be selected on the remote control device to direct the VCR to do sequences of commands packaged together. The sequences could be done by pushing various buttons one after the other, but as everyone knows, remote control devices are notoriously complicated, and it is easy to make mistakes while pushing buttons in sequence. The choice of packaged commands presented on the screen represents the manufacturer's prediction as to which sequences a typical consumer would find useful. On one such system the following choices are presented:

> Play - Rew - Power Off
> Go to Zero - Stop
> Go to Zero - Play
> Go to Rec Start - Play
> Rew - Power Off
> Rew - Eject - Power Off
> Rew - Play
> Rew - Timer Rec

It turns out that for me only five of these sequences are ever selected, reflecting my particular style of use. Other owners of the same brand might very well select different sequences, based on their most familiar patterns of use. Actually, I would very much like to have an additional one:

Go to Zero - Timer Rec

That sequence is not there, most likely reflecting a pattern of use that the manufacturer did not anticipate. There are a great many sequences one might choose to present on the screen.

In the VCR/TV context, after a sequence is selected, typically by positioning an indicator on the screen and then pressing a button, the internal computer interprets the selected sequence, simulating the less desirable method of separate button pushes by the consumer. In the programming context, the usual treatment of macros is for the programmer to write the name of the macro as a statement in the source program. Then the source language translator substitutes for the macro name the actual sequence of instructions specified in an earlier definition of the macro. Note that not only does the person who specifies the macro choose which macros to create, but also the sequence of instructions to use in the definition of each macro.[10] This is one of the areas in programming in which there is a great deal of choice, and different people solving a programming problem independently are likely to come up with very different choices of which macros would be useful, and what their definitions should be.

Parameters

A second issue concerns a programming concept that was mentioned earlier in this appendix — the subroutine, often called a procedure. The name of the subroutine, such as readln, is used to invoke its action, and the instructions in the subroutine are then executed. When the subroutine finishes its computation, control returns to the original program at the point from which the subroutine was invoked, or called. A subroutine may be called any number of times by another program, each time from a different point in the calling program. Moreover, each time it is called, it may be given different data on which to work; that is, different parameters may be specified.

One example of this, outside the context of computers, is found in a bank. We expect to be able to carry out a variety of transactions when we interact with the staff of a bank. If we approach a teller with a collection of transaction requests, we would have filled out a deposit slip for each deposit, a withdrawal slip for each withdrawal, and so on. Each type of form used triggers an appropriate action, and when that action has been completed, the next form is examined and interpreted, and the required combination of actions is carried out.

Note that, in the bank example, along with the triggering of the action by the presence of the deposit slip the specific amounts to be deposited are shown on the slip, so the deposit action is customized to the details of that deposit occurrence. That information plays the role of the parameters needed for that transaction, giving us great flexibility. It would be foolish for the bank to create a deposit slip that could only be used for one amount.

To take an example from the computing context, one frequently used subroutine in mathematical computation is the calculation of a square root. Every standard library of pre-packaged subroutines includes a subroutine for the square root, usually called SQRT, and invoked as

SQRT(x)

which means: call the square root subroutine, and specify that this time the square root of the value of the variable x is desired. Of course, another time the square root of a different value might be wanted. The variable x is referred to as the parameter.

More complicated situations require more complex parameters, even sequences of several parameters. Suppose that we wished to embed the loan amortization program that we saw earlier into a larger context, such as a program that might include various pre-payment plans, or one that would try to match the conditions of a loan to the specific characteristics of the borrower in some way. We would change the loan amortization program slightly in form, so that it would no longer be a stand-alone program, but would satisfy the format and other requirements of a subroutine. One of those requirements is the specification of the required parameters, including the order in which they would be listed, their internal storage representation (such as character, integer, etc.), whether they could be changed legitimately by the subroutine or whether any attempt to change their values should be regarded as an error, and so on. In the case of that particular program, we would no longer ask the human user to:

ENTER BALANCE, RATE, STARTING MONTH, YEAR, ENDING MONTH, YEAR, MONTHLY PAYMENT

We would instead list those required pieces of information as the necessary parameters in the call:[11]

CALL LOAN-AMORTIZATION (BALANCE, RATE, STARTING MONTH, YEAR, ENDING MONTH, YEAR, MONTHLY PAYMENT)

There are many choices to be made now. One choice is whether to specify the interest rate as an annual rate or a monthly rate. Another choice might be to always start with the current date as the starting date, because the program in which this is to be embedded might need that condition satisfied in every case. Still another choice is the order in which to list the parameters in the defining specification. There is actually a choice prior to all of these: whether to make the subroutine perform only a loan amortization, or additional functions that could be profitably done at the same time, and that could be expected to be needed most of the time by the calling program.

The point here is that there are many choices to be made, even in as mathematical a problem as this one. There were choices in selecting which computations to package into subroutines, which variables to specify as parameters, which order to list them in the description, and so on. If we find two programmers using identical parameter lists on identically specified subroutine collections, we may well wonder if they had worked independently. They probably would have made some of the choices differently. In less mathematical applications, the variety of choices is even greater.

Microcode

An issue that has only recently been resolved by a court decision is the copyrightability of microcode. What is microcode, and why is it a desirable component in computers?

It has happened that a large and expensive computer was already in production when the computer manufacturer discovered that someone had made a mistake in its design, and certain basic operations, such as multiplication, did not always give the correct result. For some particular data values, the results were a little off. Their experts looked into the problem, and they found that one of the data values involved sometimes was not getting to the required register in the ALU quickly enough to be used in the multiplication. The value that was previously in that register was being used instead. What could they do about it? It would take months to redesign the entire circuitry involved in that complex operation and make sure that it worked correctly. They would also have to make sure that it did not affect any other operation that happened to make use of part of that circuitry. All of this would make the delivery of the computer far later than promised. What they needed was to be able to change the interpretation of that particular multiplication operation, and it would need to be done in such a way that no other operation was affected.

In a different context, the designer of a new computer usually would leave a number of the possible operation codes unused in order to be able to adjust to unforeseen circumstances. Later, when the computer was in use, and the pattern of customers' programs became more apparent, certain very desirable operation codes could be "built in" by assigning them as yet unused operation codes.

The kind of flexibility needed in both of these situations is available with microcode. Instead of wiring in the behavior of the control unit so it cannot be changed, one treats the control unit as if it were a small computer within the overall computer, and then programs the control computer to interpret operation codes. This kind of programming for the inner computer is called microprogramming, and the instructions for that inner computer are called microinstructions, or microcode. With microcode, changes or additions to the behavior of the control unit, such as the proper interpretation of old or new operation codes, can be made by changing the microprogram instead of redesigning a major part of the hardware. This was, in fact, the way that the errant multiplication operation was corrected.

Let us look at the concept of microcode in a little more detail. What exactly is the job of the control unit? Its primary responsibility is to obtain an instruction from storage, break that instruction into its components (the operation code, the address of the data on which it is to operate, the address of the location where the result is to be put, and the address of the next instruction), and then coordinate and direct the actions of the various parts of the computer system so as to carry out the intended effect of the original instruction.

Suppose the next instruction to be executed is:

Add	10045	14	23167	55012

where the number 10045 represents the address of the data to be used as one value in the addition, the number 14 indicates that Register 14 in the ALU is the place to find the other value to be added, the number 23167 indicates the storage address where the result is to be placed, and the number 55012 points to the address of the next instruction. (As we said earlier, many computers omit some of these components of the instruction, leaving the control unit to substitute some standard, or default, value instead.)

We want to be sure that values arrive at various registers at the right time, not too early and not too late; that the registers are conditioned properly to receive new values; that these values are routed through the addition device at just the right time; that the result is routed to the proper storage location; and that the storage unit is ready to receive a new value after having just sent a value to the ALU. To do all of this, there has to be a timing device, usually called the clock, which ticks off precise moments at which events may occur. The clock synchronizes the behavior of the computer by establishing a sequence of cycles, that is, periods when specific events can be initiated and assumed to be complete by the time the next cycle begins, or after a known small number of cycles. The control unit sends out the signals to other parts of the computer as to what each of them should do in each clock cycle.

For example, to carry out the addition instruction illustrated above, some hypothetical computer might require the following sequence of microinstructions:

Add:				
load	a,x	load	b,r	(1)
setup	c			(2)
add	a,b	get	next	(3)
store	c	end		(4)

that would be interpreted by the control unit as follows:

1. In parallel, load two hidden registers a and b with the contents of the location referred to in the first data field of the instruction, called x here, and having the address 10045 in the example, and in the second field, called r here, and in the example, Register 14. In this hypothetical computer, we assume that both of these actions can take place at the same time, because one refers to storage and one to the ALU, and it is possible that they use independent circuitry.

2. Send the address where the result is to be put, called the c field of the instruction, and 23167 in the example, to the storage unit so it can prepare to receive a value.

3. Send the values from the internal registers a and b to the addition unit, and at the same time start the necessary process to obtain the next instruction, by sending the address of the next instruction, in the example, 55012, to the storage unit. Because the addition does not involve the storage unit, these two independent activities can be carried out in parallel.

4. Store the result of the addition directly into the storage unit, which already has been prepared to receive a value and put it into the correct place. The second half of the last microinstruction indicates that this is the end of the microsequence. The control unit concludes the interpretation of this sequence of microinstructions and begins to interpret the next instruction, which should already be on its way to the control unit after step (3) above.

Here is an example of a possible microsequence for our hypothetical computer for the operation Add Reg to Reg:

```
Add Reg to Reg:
    load       a,r1        load       b,r2
    add        a,b         get        next
    store      r2          end
```

We do not need the setup microinstruction because we are not going to put anything into a storage location.

In a computer with microcode, someone has to work out very carefully each of the sequences of microinstructions for each different operation. We have already seen one possible microsequence for the original Add operation. Another possible microsequence for the same operation might be:

```
Add:
    load       b,x         load       a,r
    add        a,b         setup      c
    get        next        store      c
    end
```

If we assume that the end microinstruction does not consume a cycle, that is, a time step, this microsequence executes faster than the original microsequence, because the original takes four cycles and this one only three. That simple change improves performance of the computer when adding two values in this way by 25 percent. It is clear that the careful design of microcode can be very important in the performance, and hence the marketing, of a computer. It follows that a collection of carefully designed, high-performance microcode sequences constitutes valuable intellectual property, whose protection could be a real issue in the industry.

A final comment. We just observed two alternate microsequences for the interpretation of the Add operation. What we were really illustrating by these alternate microsequences was the possibility of different choices made by different microprogrammers.

With so many possible choices in writing programs, we can always expect that different people working independently will produce quite different results. On the other hand, some may argue that only one best way exists; if one comes up with the same code sequences that someone else produced, either application programs or microprograms, that similarity does not mean that one copied the other person's programs. This is one of the difficult areas in the field of copyright litigation. How different should we expect independently written programs or microprograms to be? How similar do they have to be to come to the conclusion that there was copying? What should be done if there is in fact only one way to write a sequence of instructions for some particular function in the hardware; should someone be able to protect it against use by anyone else, and thus monopolize that hardware?

NOTES

1.   Chinese and Japanese characters are so numerous they require many more combinations, and provision is usually made for 512 or more distinct characters for those languages.

2.   An example of non-random-access storage, usually referred to as sequential storage, is magnetic tape, in which the only way to reach a particular location farther out on the tape is to move the tape physically past all the information ahead of the desired location.

3.   In recent years, there has been a trend toward computers with simpler instruction sets, the so-called Reduced Instruction Set Computers (RISC). Techniques have been developed to overcome the overhead of interpreting more instructions, and many people believe that RISC computers will lead eventually to much faster machines.

4.   Recall that the operation code might indicate a test to be made to decide whether to proceed sequentially or get the next instruction from some other location in storage.

5.   In practice, most programmers use an octal or hexadecimal representation for binary values, because these forms are more compressed and easier to write. The octal

representation is based on the number 8, and the hexadecimal on the number 16, just as the decimal representation is based on the number 10.

6.   Campbell-Kelly, M. "Programming the EDSAC," *Annals of the History of Computing* 2 (1980): 26.

7.   This is not an easy program to read, partly because it looks very algebraic, and partly because of the FORTRAN language, which is somewhat intimidating. The Pascal version of this program, which is shown later in this chapter, is much more friendly.

8.   Information that would appear on the user's display screen will be shown here in bold-face form.

9.   The "1" preceding the word ENTER in the Format statement causes printing to start on a new page if it were sent to a printer. We need not be concerned with that level of detail.

10.   More powerful macro facilities even provide for the specification of parameter values at each invocation of the macro, causing specific changes to occur during the substitution of the instruction sequence, and thus tailoring the sequence to the actual context in which it is invoked.

11.   The statement that follows does not conform precisely to the rules of the FORTRAN language. That detail is not important here.

REFERENCES

Sammet, J. E., *Programming Languages: History and Fundamentals* (Englewood Cliffs, N.J.: Prentice-Hall, Inc., 1969).

Appendix B:
An Example of a Patent

United States Patent [19]

Queen

[11] Patent Number: 4,807,182

[45] Date of Patent: Feb. 21, 1989

[54] **APPARATUS AND METHOD FOR COMPARING DATA GROUPS**

[75] Inventor: Cary L. Queen, Rockville, Md.

[73] Assignee: Advanced Software, Inc., Sunnyvale, Calif.

[21] Appl. No.: 839,326

[22] Filed: Mar. 12, 1986

[51] Int. Cl.^{4} G06F 15/00
[52] U.S. Cl. 364/900
[58] Field of Search ... 340/721; 364/419, 200 MS File, 364/900 MS File

[56] **References Cited**

U.S. PATENT DOCUMENTS

4,204,206	5/1980	Bakula et al.	340/721
4,212,077	7/1980	Vittorelli	364/900
4,531,201	7/1985	Skinner, Jr.	364/900
4,641,274	2/1987	Swank	364/900
4,701,745	10/1987	Waterworth	364/900

FOREIGN PATENT DOCUMENTS

0241156	11/1985	Japan	364/419
0075925	4/1986	Japan	.
0138364	6/1986	Japan	.

Primary Examiner—Gareth D. Shaw
Assistant Examiner—Viet Q. Nguyen
Attorney, Agent, or Firm—Hecker & Harriman

[57] **ABSTRACT**

Method and apparatus for comparing original and modified versions of a document. The system of the present invention utilizes a hash number generator CPU to generate hash numbers for lines and sentences contained in the documents. Matching hash numbers are defined as anchorpoints and stored in an anchorpoint memory. A comparator CPU performs a character-by-character comparison of the respective documents radiating outward from each anchorpoint. This comparison generates identity blocks which are defined as blocks which are the same in both documents. Non-identity blocks are defined as difference blocks and are characterized as insertions or deletions depending on their status. A portion of the original and modified document is displayed in a split-screen format on a display, such as a CRT. Cursors on the top and bottom half of the screen identify corresponding portions of the documents. The second cursor is generated by taking advantage of the timer interrupt sequence of a CPU to direct the CPU to program instructions to generate the second cursor.

22 Claims, 2 Drawing Sheets

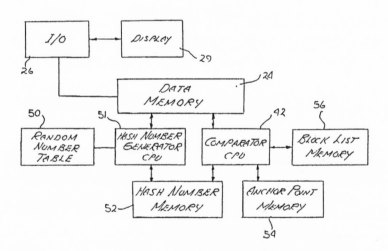

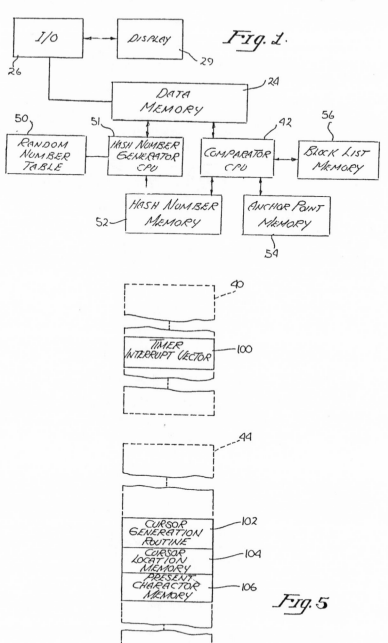

Fig. 1.

Fig. 5

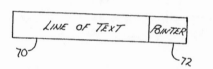

Fig. 2

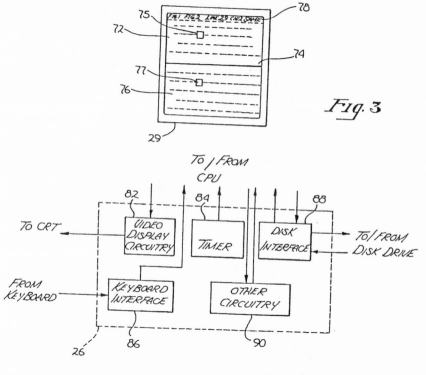

Fig. 3

Fig. 4

4,807,182

1

APPARATUS AND METHOD FOR COMPARING DATA GROUPS

BACKGROUND OF THE INVENTION

1. Field of the Invention

This invention relates generally to text processing systems and, more specifically, to a system for automatically ascertaining and isolating differences between text files, such as, for example, alphanumeric character text files.

2. Prior Art

One of the most common uses for computer systems, particularly micro computers, is text processing. Text processing typically involves the use of editors or other computer programs to create or modify files consisting of alphanumeric characters. Two major classes of text processing are "word processing", which is directed to producing standard alphanumeric documents, and "program editing" which produces lines of program source code resembling English text.

An important advantage of using a microprocessor-based system for text processing is the ability to edit easily and to revise documents. Words, sentences (such as text sentences, program lines, or character strings) or entire blocks of text are easily inserted, deleted, changed or moved using text processing systems. Use of these editing capabilities typically results in a revised file which may include much of the same material as the original file. However, it may also be rearranged or altered physically such that the two files are substantially different when perceptible copies or visual representations of both are compared. As further revisions are made, specific differences between the original and subsequent versions become increasingly difficult to identify.

To make the process of comparing different versions of program documents or character groups less difficult, systems have been developed that compare the contents of two text files and, if differences are found, indicate this fact to the user. These systems were originally developed for comparison of program source code files, though they are now frequently used when comparing English language or other high level language documents. Such prior art systems, however, suffer several major drawbacks.

A major shortcoming of the operation of prior art comparison systems is that the comparisons are made as line by line comparisons of the text in the two files. This approach is acceptable for editing of certain program code, where each line is discrete and text does not wrap around the end of lines. It is not sufficient, however, to adequately compare other types of document files. Standard documents, such as letters or reports produced by word processors. consist of sentences which often extend beyond the end of one line and continue to the following line. Thus, insertion of even a single word or character in a line may cause the end of that line to be pushed onto the subsequent line, thereby causing all of the following lines to be shifted. A text comparison system which operates line by line may detect and identify an initial addition or deletion, but it will also detect and identify all subsequent lines that have been shifted down and therefore changed. This result is clearly undesirable and inaccurate, since this latter text has not in fact been changed, but rather has merely shifted *position*.

2

Another major flaw in prior art text comparison systems is that they generally produce as output only a listing of the lines that differ between the two files. Though the user may view both the original and the changed text, he cannot view that text in proper context in the document. Further, since such prior art comparison systems only print out the text of the *differing* line, and perhaps a few surrounding lines, it is often difficult or impossible to ascertain exactly what specific changes (e.g., insertions or deletions) resulted in the displayed differences between the files. This is particularly true where line shifting, as described above, has occurred.

SUMMARY OF THE INVENTION

The present invention provides methods and apparatus which permit identification of specific differences between two character files, (e.g., text files) and simultaneously display of those differences in the context in which they occur. In addition, the nature of the change that creates the difference (e.g., insertion, deletion or movement of text) is specifically identified.

In accordance with the presently preferred embodiment of this invention, means are provided for copying the text of the two documents to be compared into memory. Each line and sentence in the first document is then converted into a number using a process known as hashing. These numbers are stored in a list in memory, along with the location of that line or sentence in the first document.

The hashing process is then repeated for each line and sentence in the second document. As each resulting number is generated, it is compared with numbers derived from the first document. Where the numbers match in both documents, this fact is recorded, along with the position of the matching line/sentence, in the second document.

For each of the matching numbers from the two documents, the text at the recorded locations is compared to generate the largest possible block of identity. When an identity block of at least a specified minimum size is found, it is recorded in memory along with its location in both documents. After this process is completed for all of the matching numbers, the remaining text, which differs between the two documents, is broken into "difference blocks". For each difference block, the above steps are repeated on short phrases rather than lines or sentences to produce a finer level of comparison. The identity blocks are then classified as either "same" blocks or "moved" blocks depending on whether the relative positions of text in the two documents is the same. Difference blocks are also classified, where appropriate, as either "deletion" or "insertion" blocks if the text is missing from one of the original files.

Finally, the text of both documents is displayed simultaneously on a CRT or other suitable output device in small segments. The user is free to use the keyboard to position the cursor anywhere in the first document, and a second cursor is automatically placed in the corresponding location in the second document. Further, the display indicates whether the text currently being viewed is the same or has been changed, moved, inserted or deleted in the second document.

The preferred embodiment of the present invention includes means for reading the documents to be compared, storing the documents in memory, making a comparison and displaying text. Further, logic means are provided for hashing and comparing of the docu-

4,807,182

ments as well as for displaying documents simultaneously.

BRIEF DESCRIPTION OF THE DRAWINGS

FIG. 1 is a block diagram of the apparatus of the present invention.

FIG. 2 illustrates the storage structure for lines of text stored in the memory in the present invention.

FIG. 3 illustrates a typical display produced by the present invention.

FIG. 4 is a block diagram of I/O circuitry of the present invention.

FIG. 5 illustrates a typical arrangement of the elements of the display routine within the memory of in the present invention.

DETAILED DESCRIPTION OF THE INVENTION

Notation and Nomenclature

The detailed description which follows is presented largely in terms of algorithms and symbolic representations of operations on data bits within a computer memory. The algorithmic descriptions and representations are the means used by those skilled in the data processing arts to most effectively convey the substance of their work to others skilled in the art.

An algorithm is here, and generally, conceived to be a self-consistent sequence of steps leading to a desired result. These steps are those requiring physical manipulations of physical quantities. Usually, though not necessarily, these quantities take the form of electrical or magnetic signals capable of being stored, transferred, combined, compared and otherwise manipulated. It proves convenient at times, principally for reasons of common usage, to refer to these signals as bits, values, elements, symbols, characters, terms, numbers, or the like. It should be kept in mind, however, that all of these and similar terms are to be associated with the appropriate physical quantities and are merely convenient labels applied to these quantities.

Further, the manipulations performed are often referred to in terms, (such as adding or comparing) which are commonly associated with mental operations performed by a human operator. No such capability of a human operator is necessary, or desirable in most cases, in any of the operations described herein which form art of the present invention; the operations are machine operations. Useful machines for performing the operations of the present invention include general purpose digital computers or other similar devices. In all cases the distinction between the method of operations and operating a computer, and the method of computation itself should be noted. The present invention relates to methods of operating a computer in processing electrical or other (e.g., mechanical, chemical) physical signals to generate other desired physical signals.

The present invention also relates to apparatus for performing these operations. This apparatus may be specially constructed for the required purposes or it may comprise a general purpose computer as selectively activated or reconfigured by a computer program stored in the computer. The algorithms presented herein are not inherently related to any particular computer or other apparatus. In particular, various general purpose machines may be used with the teachings herein, or it may prove more convenient to construct more specialized apparatus to perform the required method steps. The required structure for a variety of

these machines will appear from the description given below.

In addition, in the following description, numerous details are set forth such as algorithmic conventions, specific numbers of bits, etc., in order to provide a thorough understanding of the present invention. However it will be apparent to one skilled in the art that the present invention may be practiced without these specific details. In other instances, well-known circuits and structures are not described in detail in order not to obscure the present invention unnecessarily.

DETAILED DESCRIPTION

The following detailed description is divided into several sections. The first of these discloses the general configuration of a system for comparing documents. Later sections address specific aspects of the present invention, including means for identifying corresponding block of text in two files, ascertaining changes in text blocks, and providing output of the results of the comparison.

GENERAL SYSTEM CONFIGURATION

FIG. 1 is a block diagram illustrating the preferred embodiment to the present invention. The system includes Input/Output (I/O) means 26, data/system memory 24, random number table 50, hash number generator CPU 51, comparator CPU 42, block list memory 56, hash number memory 52, anchorpoint memory 54 and display 29.

Groups of data to be compared are entered into the system through the I/O 26. In the preferred embodiment of the present invention, the system is used to compare drafts of documents and this description is written in regard to document comparison. It will be understood, however, that the system may be utilized to compare any two groups of data or characters that are capable of storage in a memory. An original and modified version of the subject document is stored in the data/system memory 24. In the preferred embodiment of the present invention, the data/system memory consists of a Random Access Memory (RAM).

TEXT STORAGE AND HASHING

Each document stored in data/system memory 24 consists of lines of alphanumeric characters represented by binary codes. In general practice, codes of 7 or 8 bits for each character are used. Thus, in addition to upper and lower case letters and numerals, a number of punctuation and special purpose marks can also be stored. Various coding schemes, such as IBM Extended AS-CII, (8 bits) may be used.

In order to more efficiently utilize memory, the lines of each document are stored as a linked list, as depicted in FIG. 2. For each line of text 70 stored, a pointer 72 is also stored. This pointer contains the address in data/system memory 24 where the next line is stored. Utilizing this scheme, data/system memory 24 need not consist of a contiguous block of memory large enough for each document, but may be made up of numerous small blocks, located wherever memory is available, and chained together in the linked list. The memory location in data/system memory 24 of the first line in each file is saved at a known location so that the contents of the files may be retrieved.

Although any two text files can be compared using this invention, a frequent use is to compare two versions

4,807,182

5

of the same document or program. As noted, for purposes of this discussion, it is assumed that such a comparison is being made. For convention and clarity, the original (unmodified) document will be referred to as file 1 and the later (modified) version as file 2. Of course, in practice it is left to the user to specify which of the files is to be considered the original version and which the modified version. Reversal of the two files will not affect the comparison process, though text which was inserted may be identified as deleted and vice versa.

Once the text of both files has been stored in data/system memory, each line of file 1 is converted to a number by hashing. In the preferred embodiment of the present invention, the hashing process is performed by a hash number generator CPU 51 coupled to data/system memory 24. Although any number of currently available microprocessors can serve as hash number generator CPU 51, the 8086/88 family of microprocessors, manufactured by Intel Corporation of Santa Clara, Calif. are particularly well suited for use with the present invention. In operation, the hash number generator CPU retrieves a line of text from data/system memory 24. The binary code value of the first character in the line (a number from 0 to 255) is taken as the base hash value. The value of the following character is then used as an index into random number table 50, coupled to hash number generator CPU 51 and containing 256 random numbers in the preferred embodiment. The value stored at the location indexed by the second character of the line is combined with the base hash value by applying an exclusive OR (XOR) function. The XOR function is defined such that each bit in the result will be set to 1 if the corresponding bit in one, but not both, of the original bytes is set to 1. The result of this XOR becomes the temporary hash value.

This process is then repeated for each subsequent character in the line, using it as an index into the random number table 50 and generating a new temporary hash value by XORing the random number retrieved with the previous temporary hash value. The result after the last character in the line is processed is the final hash number.

This final hash number is then stored in hash number memory 52, along with the location in the file, by line number, of the line from which this number was generated. Hash number memory 52 is coupled to hash number generator CPU 51. This process is repeated for each remaining line until all lines have been converted into hash numbers. The same procedure is then repeated for the entire file again, sentence by sentence (rather than line by line). With sentences, the location information (stored along with the hash number in hash number memory 52), includes both the line number and position within the line of the first character in the sentence. At the completion of this process, hash number memory 52 will contain a hash number and location data for each line and each sentence in file 1.

It should be noted that hashing described above is designed such that identical lines or sentences will have identical hash numbers. Due to the nature of hashing it is also possible, though not likely, for two different line or sentences to have the same hash number, which is known as a collision. However, this possibility is substantially minimized by use of the random number table 50. The entries in this table can either be generated by the computer or included as part of a document comparison routine. Though an excessive number of colli-

6

sions will tend to reduce the comparison speed, accuracy of the results will not be affected, as will be seen in the discussion of the identity block identification procedure below.

Next, the above hashing process is repeated for the text of file 2. However, as each hash number from file 2 is generated, it is compared with the hash numbers from file 1 in hash number memory 52, rather than being stored. For purposes of efficiency, hash numbers generated from lines need only be compared with hash numbers from lines and hash numbers from sentences with hash numbers from other sentences. This comparison is performed by comparator CPU 42 which is coupled to data/system memory 24, hash number memory 52 and hash number generator CPU 51. In the preferred embodiment, comparator CPU 42 comprises a microprocessor such as an Intel 8086/88 type of microprocessor. Although hash number generator CPU 51 and comparator CPU 42 are shown as separate processors in FIG. 1, a single microprocessor may be utilized to perform both functions. By way of example, the Intel 8086/88 family is capable of performing both functions.

Each match between the hash number from file 2 and a hash number from file 1 is called an "anchorpoint" and is copied to anchorpoint memory 54, along with the location of the corresponding line or sentence in each file. Anchorpoint memory 54 is coupled to comparator CPU 42.

IDENTITY BLOCK IDENTIFICATION

The anchorpoints generated as described above contain the locations in each file of the beginning of a segment of text which matched in both Files. In order to speed comparison, these segments of matching text are expanded as much as possible. The result is the creation of "identity blocks" of text which are the same in both files, generated as follows:

For each anchorpoint stored in anchorpoint memory 54, the text location in each file is identified. The size of the block of matching text is then expanded by performing a character-by-character comparison of the text of both files, radiating outward from the anchorpoint. This comparison is performed by comparator CPU 42. Comparator CPU 42 is coupled to data/system memory 24. After reading an anchorpoint from anchorpoint memory 54, comparator CPU 42 locates the text location in data/system memory 24. Comparator CPU 42 then undertakes a character-by-character comparison of the matching text on either side of the anchorpoint. Thus, if the anchorpoint represents text at some point X in file 1 and identical text at some point Y in file 2, the $(X+1)$th character is compared with the $(Y+1)$th character, then the $(X+2)$th with the $(Y+2)$th, and so on until they fail to match. The point where the difference occurs becomes one end of the identity block. However, if this difference occurs within the body of a word, the end of the identity block is taken to be the last character of the preceeding word. This character by character comparison is then repeated in the reverse direction, starting again at the anchorpoint and comparing the $(X-1)$th character with the $(Y-1)$th character, and so on, until they no longer match. When these comparisons are complete, the beginning and end points, in both files, of an identity block containing the original anchorpoint will have been identified.

If the identity block is below a set minimum size, M_{ib} (20 non-blank characters in the presently preferred embodiment) it is ignored. This will normally be the case if

4,807,182

the anchorpoint was created by a hash collison rather than lines or sentences that match. Otherwise, the location information and a notation that this is an identity block are stored in block list memory 56, coupled to comparator CPU 42. Any anchorpoints contained within the boundaries of identity block are deleted from anchorpoint memory 54. The above-described block extension process is then repeated for each anchorpoint remaining in anchorpoint memory 54, until all anchorpoints have been deleted by being converted to identity blocks or by being found within an identity block.

OVERLAP ELIMINATION

In the case where a block of text from file 1 appears more frequently in file 2, an overlap of identity blocks will occur. For example, if a quotation which appears only once in file 1 is used twice in file 2, the identity blocks generated will overlap, with both blocks covering a portion of the same text. This can result in one of the text blocks being improperly identified as present in File when it in fact was not.

Overlapping blocks are eliminated by associating one of the blocks from file 2 with the identical block in file 1, and reclassifying the remaining blocks from file 2 as difference (insertion) blocks.

This is accomplished by using paragraphs or sentence breaks in the text to determine which of the blocks in file 2 should be associated with the identical block from file 1. Thus text which appears within the same sentence or paragraph as the block in question will be deemed to correspond. Duplicate blocks found outside of the paragraph or sentence in question are reclassified as difference blocks.

DIFFERENCE BLOCK IDENTIFICATION

After all of the identity blocks have been established, according to the above procedure, text which differs between the two files will not be included in any identity blocks. This remaining text is broken into "difference blocks", separated naturally by the identity blocks.

Specifically, each section of different text from file 1 is associated with the corresponding different text at the same relative location in file 2 to form a difference block. This block information is then stored in block list memory 56, along with a notation that it is a difference block, in the same manner as with the identity blocks.

FINER COMPARISON

To provide a finer level of comparison, the text within each difference block is subjected to the method described above, including hashing anchorpoint identification and identity/difference block identification. However, on this pass the hashing is applied to short groups of words or phrases, rather than to entire sentences or lines. In addition, the minimum size required to process an identity block, M_{ib} is also reduced. The method otherwise proceeds as previously described, without the need to read data into memory since the text making up the difference blocks is already present in memory.

After this second phase is completed, the original difference blocks are broken into groups of smaller differences and identity blocks all stored in block list memory 56. The method is then repeated on any remaining difference blocks. In the preferred embodiment of the present invention, these iterative comparisons are thereby hashing on successively smaller groups of characters, until no further blocks of identical text can be

found in the preferred embodiment within the difference blocks. However, the iterative method stops when identity blocks become smaller than 5 characters.

BLOCK CLASSIFICATION

After all identity blocks and difference blocks have been identified and stored in block list memory 56, the list is examined to further classify the blocks. Each identity block is classified as a "moved" block if the text is not located in the same relative position in both files. Otherwise, it is marked as a "same" block.

Certain difference blocks are classified as either "insertion" or "deletion" blocks by examining the text at the locations in each file stored in block list memory 56. If the relative location in file 2 of the text block in file 1 contains only blank space, the block is marked as a "deletion" block. If file 1 contains only blank space which corresponds to text in file 2, the block is then marked as an "insertion" block. In the case where both files have non-blank text, the block simply remains marked as a difference block.

DISPLAY OF RESULTS

When identification and classification of blocks is completed, the text of both files is displayed simultaneously, with the differences between them indicated. In the presently preferred embodiment, display 29 is a CRT and is capable of displaying up to 25 lines of text at one time, and each file is displayed 11 lines at a time. FIG. 3 shows the state of this display at a given instant.

Eleven lines of text, (initially the first eleven) from file 1 are copied from data/system memory 24 (FIG. 1) to top half 72 (FIG. 2) of CRT 29. A dividing line 74, consisting of a row of any suitable character (a solid block character in the present embodiment) is displayed on line 13 of display 29 to divide the display. The 11 lines from file 2 that correspond to the 11 displayed lines of file 1 according to the block structure, are copied from data memory 24 and displayed on bottom half 76 of CRT 29. The top line 78 of the CRT is reserved for display of status messages to the user, including the names of the files being compared, the current location in the document, and the nature of the text being examined (e.g., same, inserted, deleted, different, moved).

For each character on the screen, the block containing that character is determined by examining block list memory 56. If the character is in a difference, insertion, deletion or moved block but not a same block, the character is brightened on display 29 using I/O circuitry 26. Hence all text on the screen that has been changed in any way is highlighted by brightening and thus made readily apparent.

In addition to the text display, a cursor is displayed on each half of the CRT 29. The upper cursor 75 is controlled by the user. User commands are interpreted to allow the cursor to be positioned on any character in file 1. When the cursor is moved to a position in the file beyond those lines presently displayed, the text displayed on top half 72 is scrolled up or down accordingly, so that the text under the cursor is always visible. If necessary, the text on bottom half 76 is then also scrolled to maintain its correspondence with top half 72. Lower cursor 77, displayed on bottom half 76 of the display 29 is not under user control, but follows the motion of upper cursor 75. Specifically, lower cursor 77 is always over the character in file 2 that corresponds to the character under upper cursor 75 in file 1, i.e., lower cursor 77 is over the character in file 2 that is in the

4,807,182

same identity or difference block as the character in file 1 and is at the same relative position in that block.

At each position of upper cursor 75, the identity/difference block which contains the character underneath the cursor is identified by examining block list memory 56. When the block containing the character at that location is located, the categorization information for that block (i.e. same, different, inserted, deleted or moved) is extracted from block list memory 56 and an appropriate message is displayed on Top Line 78. Thus, as the user moves the Upper Cursor 75 through file 1, he is not only able to simultaneously view the corresponding text in file 2, but is continuously apprised of the nature of the difference between the two files at the current location. If the user gives an appropriate command, the upper cursor 75 will automatically be placed at the beginning of the next difference block. Therefore, the user can move from change to change in the files while skipping over unchanged text.

Although, in the preferred embodiment, a CRT is utilized as display 29, other types of display may be advantageously utilized with the present invention. For example, display 29 may comprise a printer. When the present invention is utilized with a printer, the user may select a printout of the original document, modified document or both. When a printout is provided, sections that have been inserted into the original document may be identified by underlining. Deleted sections may be identified by placing a caret at the beginning and end of the deleted passage. Changed passages may be identified with the use of a caret in conjunction with underlining. It will be understood, that the above methods of printout are given by way of example only, and any suitable means of identifying changes in the document may be utilized.

SECOND CURSOR GENERATION

Lower cursor 77, usually displayed as a flashing underscore, is generated by the video display circuitry 82 (FIG. 4) portion of I/O circuitry 26, under control of comparator CPU 42 (FIG. 1). However, most micro computer systems provide no means for displaying a second cursor, upper cursor 75, which is necessary to the above-disclosed simultaneous display method. The present invention overcomes this shortcoming by utilizing a CPU timer interrupt to generate a second cursor.

As shown in FIG. 4, I/O Circuitry 26 contains hardware timer 84, which usually consists of a fixed frequency oscillator and counter circuits. These devices are configured such that a signal is generated at regular intervals (18.5 times each second in the preferred embodiment). This signal is known as the "timer interrupt" and is coupled to interrupt lines on CPU 22 such that each time the timer interrupt signal is asserted, the CPU completes the current instruction, saves its present location and register information, and jumps to a predetermined location.

This location, known as timer interrupt vector 100, is shown in FIG. 5 as part of data/system memory 24 (FIG. 1). Instructions stored at timer interrupter vector 100 cause the CPU 42 (FIG. 1) to begin executing cursor generation routine 102 (FIG. 5), which is located within data/system memory 24 (FIG. 1). Cursor location 104 contains the desired location for upper cursor 75 at any given time. Cursor character 106 contains a copy of the character in file 1 at the same relative location as specified in cursor location 104.

To generate the upper cursor 75, a suitable character is chosen to be displayed as a cursor. In the presently preferred embodiment this is the solid block character which is available under IBM Extended ASCII. When the cursor generation routine 102 is first entered, the character displayed on top half 72 (FIG. 3) at the cursor location 104 is replaced on the display with the solid block character. The cursor generation routine then exits and the CPU returns from the timer interrupt to continue processing, or to execute other routines triggered by the timer interrupt.

On the following timer interrupt, providing the upper cursor 75 has not moved (which would be indicated by a new location in cursor location 104) the solid block character is replaced with the original character in that location, stored in cursor character 106. If the cursor has been moved since the last timer interrupt, then the character from the previous location is restored from cursor character 106 and the character at the present cursor location is saved in cursor character 106 and replaced by the solid block character. The cursor generation routine 102 again exits to await the next timer interrupt. This process of alternating the actual character at the upper cursor 75 location and the solid block is continued indefinitely with the actual location of the cursor display changing as the upper cursor 75 is moved by the user.

It should be noted that because of the relatively high frequency of the timer interrupt, alternating characters on each interrupt may not provide a pleasing display. In order to compensate for this, the solid block and the character under upper cursor 75 may in fact be swapped less frequently, perhaps once every several timer interrupts, to achieve a more pleasant result. Further, the amount of time during which the solid block is displayed need not be equal to that during which the underlying character is displayed. In the presently preferred embodiment, it has been found that the most desirable display is achieved by displaying the solid block for 2 timer interrupts, followed by the underlying character for 4 timer interrupts, followed again by the block for 2 interrupts and so on.

CODING DETAILS

No particular programming language has been indicated for carrying out the various procedures described above. This is in part due to the fact that not all languages that might be mentioned are universally available. Each user of a particular computer will be aware of the language which is most suitable for his immediate purpose. In practice, it has proven useful to implement the present invention in a combination of 8088 Assembly Language and PASCAL.

Because the computers which may be used in practicing the instant invention consist of may diverse elements and devices, no detailed program listings have been provided. It is considered that the operations and other procedures described above and illustrated in the accompanying drawings are sufficiently disclosed to permit one of ordinary skill in the art to practice the instant invention or so much of it as is of use to him.

Thus, methods and apparatus which are most advantageously used in conjunction with a digital computer and related peripheral devices to provide automated comparison and simultaneous display of two documents have been disclosed. The present invention's use of hashing on sentences and phrases and identity/difference block identification provides a degree of accuracy

4,807,182

11

and convenience unavailable in the prior art. Further, the means provided for generating a second cursor allow a simultaneous display not found in the prior art.

While the present invention has been particularly described with reference to FIGS. 1–5 and with empha- 5 sis on certain computer systems and peripheral devices, it should be understood that the figures are for illustration only and should not be taken as limitations upon the invention. In addition, it is clear that the methods and apparatus of the present invention have utility in any 10 application where automatic test comparison is desired. It is contemplated that many changes and modifications may be made, by one of ordinary skill in the art, without departing from the spirit and scope of the invention as described above.   15

I claim:

1. An automated comparison system, comprising:

input means for receiving commands, and for providing electronic signals representing a plurality of characters including words and sentences;   20

memory means coupled to said input means for storing as binary representations at least first and second groups of said characters;

processing means coupled to said memory means and to said input means for detecting and indentifying 25 differences between said words and sentences first and second groups of said characters;

display means coupled to said processing means for providing a display of said differences.

2. The system of claim 1 wherein said processing 30 means includes reading means for reading and comparing said first and second groups of characters from said memory means.

3. The system of claim 2 wherein said processing 35 means includes writing means for writing said groups of characters from said memory means to said display means.

4. The system of claim 3 wherein said processing means includes first logic means for generating hash 40 numbers, said hash numbers being derived said binary representations of said characters in said first and second groups of characters such that identical groups of characters will result in identical hash numbers.

5. The system of claim 4 wherein said processing 45 means includes comparison means for comparing hash numbers generated from sentences, words and characters of said first and second groups.

6. The system of claim 5 wherein said processing means includes second logic means for creating lists of 50 data in said memory means.

7. The system of claim 6 wherein said processing means includes searching means for identifying and retrieving selected information from said lists of data.

8. The system of claim 7 wherein said processing 55 means includes interrupt detection means for detecting the presence of an interrupt signal and transferring control to a selected location in said memory means.

9. The system of claim 8 wherein said processing means further includes timer means for generating a 60 signal at designated intervals.

10. The system of claim 1 wherein said display means comprises a Cathode Ray Tube.

11. The system of claim 1 wherein said display means comprises a printer.   65

12. A method for identifying and displaying the differences between first and second documents, said documents comprising groups of alphanumeric characters

12

including words, lines and sentences comprising the steps of:

storing each of said documents in a memory;

generating hash numbers from said lines and sentences of each of said documents, such that identical lines and identical sentences produce identical corresponding hash numbers;

comparing hash numbers generated for said first document with hash numbers generated from said second document;

creating lists of anchorpoints in said memory, said anchorpoints representing matching hash numbers from each of said documents;

defining blocks of identical text in both documents containing at least one anchorpoint;

defining difference blocks of text not contained in said identity blocks;

storing in memory the location in each document of said identity and difference blocks;

classifying said identity and difference blocks into one of a plurality of classifications and storing said classifications in memory;

displaying said identity and difference blocks and said classifications.

13. The method as defined by claim 12 further comprising the step of defining identity blocks by comparison of the characters in each document radiating outward from said anchorpoints.

14. The method as defined by claim 13 further comprising the step of deleting from memory all anchorpoints contained within each of said identity blocks.

15. The method as defined by claim 14 further comprising the step of associating a location of difference blocks in said first document with a correspoonding location in said second document.

16. The method as defined by claim 15 further comprising the step of repeating all above steps on successively smaller blocks or characters within said difference blocks to identify small identity blocks within said difference blocks.

17. The method as defined by claim 16 wherein said small identity blocks comprise a selected number of characters.

18. The method as defined by claim 17 further comprising the step of stimultaneously displaying selected portions of each document.

19. The method as defined by claim 18 further comprising the step of displaying said classifications of said identity and difference blocks.

20. The method as defined by claim 19 further comprising the step of simultaneously displaying corresponding blocks from said first and second documents.

21. In a computer controlled display system having a display wherein first and second groups of characters are simultaneously displayed and differences between said first and second groups are indicated on said display, a method for displaying said groups and said differences comprising the steps of:

generating and displaying said first group of characters on a first region of said display;

generating and displaying said second group of characters on a second region of said display;

controlling the scrolling of said first and second regions so that the group of characters in said second region correspond to the group of characters in said first region;

determining differences between said first and second groups of characters;

4,807,182

13

14

generating and displaying indicators in said first and second regions, said indicators identifying said differences between said first and second groups of characters;

whereby said first and second groups of characters and said differences are displayed.

22. The method of claim 21 further including the step

of providing first and second cursors on said display, said first cursor displayed in said first region and said second cursor displayed in said second region, the position of said second cursor corresponding to the position of said first cursor.

* * * * *

10

15

20

25

30

35

40

45

50

55

60

65

Appendix B

UNITED STATES PATENT AND TRADEMARK OFFICE
CERTIFICATE OF CORRECTION

PATENT NO. : 4,807,182
DATED : February 21, 1989
INVENTOR(S) : Cary L. Queen

It is certified that error appears in the above-identified patent and that said Letters Patent is hereby corrected as shown below:

In column 3, line 46, "art" should be changed to -- part --. at line 51, "distortion" sould be changed to --distinction--.

In column 4, line 19, change "block" to --blocks--.

In column 6, line 61, change "(x-1)the" to --(x-1)th--.

In column 10, line 48, change "availale" to --available--.

In claim 1, line 10, insert --in said-- after the word "sentences".

Signed and Sealed this

Nineteenth Day of December, 1989

Attest:

JEFFREY M. SAMUELS

Attesting Officer   *Acting Commissioner of Patents and Trademarks*

Appendix C:
A Concurring Opinion in
In re Alappat

92-1381
IN RE KURIAPPAN P. ALAPPAT, EDWARD
E. AVERILL and JAMES G. LARSEN

RADER, *Circuit Judge*, concurring.

I join Judge Rich's opinion holding that this court has subject matter jurisdiction over this appeal and reversing the reconstituted Board of Patent Appeals and Interferences' decision on the merits. While I fully agree with Judge Rich that Alappat's claimed invention falls squarely within the scope of 35 U.S.C. § 101 (1988), I write to clarify that this conclusion does not hinge on whether Alappat's invention is classified as machine or process under section 101.

The reconstituted Board determined that applicants' (Alappat's) invention is a process excluded from the subject matter of 35 U.S.C. § 101. The Board concluded that the invention is a "mathematical algorithm" rather than a patentable machine. The Board reached this conclusion by impermissibly expanding the scope of the claimed subject matter, thereby running afoul of 35 U.S.C. § 112, ¶ 6 (1988). *See In re Donaldson Co.*, 16 F.3d 1189, 1193, 29 USPQ2d 1845, 1848 (Fed. Cir. 1994) (in banc). Not surprisingly, the initial Board found no problem with 35 U.S.C. § 101 when the claims were properly interpreted in light of the specification.

Judge Rich, with whom I fully concur, reads Alappat's application as claiming a machine. In fact, whether the invention is a process or a machine is irrelevant. The language of the Patent Act itself, as well as Supreme Court rulings, clarifies that Alappat's invention fits comfortably within 35 U.S.C. § 101 whether viewed as a process or a machine.

Section 101 of the Patent Act states:

Whoever invents or discovers any new and useful process, machine, manufacture, or composition of matter, or any new and useful improvement thereof, may obtain a patent therefor, subject to the conditions and requirements of this title.

Any new and useful process, machine, article of manufacture, or composition of matter, including improvements, may thus receive patent protection. Section 101 explicitly covers both processes and machines. Furthermore, according to the Supreme Court, "any" is an expansive term encompassing "'anything under the sun that is made by man.'" *Diamond v. Chakrabarty*, 447 U.S. 303, 309 (1980) (quoting S. Rep. No. 1979, 82d Cong., 2d Sess. 5 (1952); H.R. Rep. No. 1923, 82d Cong., 2d Sess. 6 (1952)). Section 101 does not suggest that patent protection extends to some subcategories of processes or machines and not to others. The Act simply does not extend coverage to some new and useful inventions and deny it to others.

Indeed, the Supreme Court has clarified that section 101 means what it says: *any* new and useful invention is entitled to patent protection, subject to the remaining statutory conditions for patentability. See *Diamond v. Diehr*, 450 U.S. 175, 182 (1981). In determining what qualifies as patentable subject matter, the Supreme Court has drawn the distinction between inventions and mere discoveries. On the unpatentable discovery side fall "laws of nature, natural phenomena, and abstract ideas." *Diehr*, 450 U.S. at 185. On the patentable invention side fall anything that is "not nature's handiwork, but [the inventor's] own." *Chakrabarty*, 447 U.S. at 310. While Judge Rich correctly applies these principles to machines, they apply with equal force to processes.

The dividing line between patentable invention and mere discovery applies equally well to algorithmic inventions. In *Diehr*, the Court indicated that in special cases, an algorithm is tantamount to a "law of nature" and therefore non-statutory. *Diehr*, 450 U.S. at 186. However, the Court noted that "[t]he term 'algorithm' is subject to a variety of definitions." *Id.* at 186 n.9. The Court refused to expand the term "algorithm" beyond the narrow definition employed in *Gottschalk v. Benson*,

409 U.S. 63, 65 (1972) and *Parker v. Flook*, 437 U.S. 584, 589 (1978), two cases in which the Court ruled the inventions non-statutory:

[The petitioner's] definition is significantly broader than the definition this Court employed in *Benson* and *Flook*. Our previous decisions regarding the patentability of "algorithms" are necessarily limited to the more narrow definition employed by the Court, and we do not pass judgment on whether processes falling outside the definition previously used by this Court, but within the definition offered by the petitioner, would be patentable subject matter.

Diehr, 450 U.S. at 186 n.9.

Thus, in *Diehr*, the Court specifically confined the holdings of *Benson* and *Flook* to the facts of those cases. Significantly, the Court thereby refused to classify all algorithms as non-statutory subject matter. Only algorithms which merely represent discovered principles are excluded from section 101. The inventions in *Benson* and *Flook* involved such algorithms. In *Benson*, the invention was simply a way to solve a general mathematics problem; in *Flook* the invention was a way to obtain a number. *Diehr*, 450 U.S. at 185–86. In pronouncing the severe confinement of the earlier decisions, the Supreme Court restored the Patent Act's clear meaning that processes and machines are patentable subject matter even if they include an algorithm. In the wake of *Diehr* and *Chakrabarty*, the Supreme Court only denies patentable subject matter status to algorithms which are, in fact, simply laws of nature.

Moreover, "a claim drawn to subject matter otherwise statutory does not become nonstatutory simply because it uses a mathematical formula, computer program or digital computer." *Diehr*, 450 U.S. at 187. Viewing the claim as a whole, if a digital circuit or its use would define an invention under section 101, then the same invention described in terms of "a mathematical formula, computer program or digital computer" should be statutory subject matter as well. Neither Alappat's digital circuit, nor a mathematical algorithm that replaces it in a computer, is a "fundamental law of nature" excluded from the scope of section 101. In sum, section 101 is no bar to Alappat whether his invention is a machine — which it is — or a process — which it employs.

The limits on patentable subject matter within section 101 do not depend on whether an invention can be expressed as a mathematical relationship or algorithm. Mathematics is simply a form of expression — a language. As this court's predecessor pointed out:

[S]ome mathematical algorithms and formulae do not represent scientific principles or laws of nature; they represent ideas or mental processes and are simply logical vehicles for communicating possible solutions to complex problems.

In re Meyer, 688 F.2d 789, 794–95, 215 USPQ 193, 197 (CCPA 1982).

The Supreme Court's *Diehr* doctrine in effect recognizes that inventors are their own lexicographers. Therefore, inventors may express their inventions in any manner they see fit, including mathematical symbols and algorithms. Whether an inventor calls the invention a machine or a process is not nearly as important as the invention itself. Thus, the inventor can describe the invention in terms of a dedicated circuit or a process that emulates that circuit. Indeed, the line of demarcation between a dedicated circuit and a computer algorithm accomplishing the identical task is frequently blurred and is becoming increasingly so as the technology develops. In this field, a software process is often interchangeable with a hardware circuit. Thus, the Board's insistence on reconstruing Alappat's machine claims as processes is misguided when the technology recognizes no difference and the Patent Act treats both as patentable subject matter.

The Supreme Court has frequently cautioned that "courts 'should not read into the patent laws limitations and conditions which the legislature has not expressed.'" *Chakrabarty*, 447 U.S. at 308 (quoting *United States v. Dubilier Condenser Corp.*, 289 U.S. 178, 199 (1933)). This same counsel applies to the Board. The Board has no justification within the Patent Act to ignore algorithmic processes or machines as "useful Arts" within the scope of section 101. U.S. Const. art. I, § 8. This court should not permit the Patent and Trademark Office to administratively emasculate research and development in this area by precluding statutory protection for algorithmic inventions.

The applicants of the instant invention do not seek to patent a mathematical formula. They seek protection for an invention that displays a smooth line on an oscilloscope. Although Alappat's machine or process might employ an equation, it does not pre-empt that equation. Consequently, whether the invention is called a machine or a process is inconsequential. For these reasons, I agree with this court's reversal of the reconstituted Board's decision.

Appendix D:
Citations List

Note: The first term in each entry is the popular name for the case cited.

Alappat	*In re Alappat* 33 F.3d 1526 (Fed. Cir. 1994)
Allen-Myland	*Allen-Myland, Inc. v. IBM,* 770 F.Supp. 1004, 1014 (E.D.Pa. 1991)
Altai	*Computer Associates Int'l, Inc. v. Altai, Inc.,* 22 F.3d 32 (2d Cir. 1992), 8325 F. Supp. 50 (E.D.N.Y. 1993)
Arnstein	*Arnstein v. Porter,* 154 F.2d 464 (2d Cir. 1946)
Atari	*Atari Games Corp. v. Nintendo of America, Inc.,* 975 F.2d 832 (Fed. Cir. 1992)
Baker v. Selden	*Baker v. Selden,* 101 U. S. 99 (1879)
Borland	*Lotus Development Corp. v. Borland International, Inc.,* 831 F.Supp. 223 (D. Mass. 1993)
Broderbund	*Broderbund Software, Inc. v. Unison World, Inc.,* 648 F. Supp. 1127 (N. D. Cal. 1986)
Brooktree	*Brooktree Corp. v. Advanced Micro Devices, Inc.,* 977 F.2d 1555 (Fed. Cir. 1992)
Diehr	*Diamond, Commissioner of Patents and Trademarks v. Diehr,* 450 U.S. 175 (1981)

Donaldson	*In Re Donaldson Company, Inc.,* 16 F.3d 1189 (Fed. Cir. 1994)
ENIAC	*Honeywell, Inc. v. Sperry Rand Corp.,* 180 U.S.P.Q. 673, 1973 W.L. 903 (D.Minn. Oct. 19, 1973)
Feist	*Feist Publications, Inc. v. Rural Telephone Service Co., Inc.,* 499 U.S. 340 (1991)
Formula	*Apple Computer, Inc. v. Formula Int' l, Inc.,* 725 F.2d 521 (9th Cir. 1984)
Franklin	*Apple Computer, Inc. v. Franklin Computer Corp.,* 714 F.2d 1240 (3rd Cir. 1983), cert. dismissed 464 U. S. 1033 (1984)
Frybarger	*Frybarger v. International Business Machines Corporation,* 812 F.2d 525 (9th Cir. 1987)
Gates Rubber	*Gates Rubber Co. v. Bando American, Inc.,* 9 F.3rd 829 (10th Cir. 1993)
Halliburton	*Halliburton Oil Well Cementing Co. v. C. P. Walker,* 329 U.S. 1 (1946)
Intel	*NEC, Inc. v. Intel, Inc.,* 1989 W.L. 67434 (N. D. Cal. Feb. 7, 1989)
Lotus	*Lotus Development Corp. v. Paperback Software Int' l,* 740 F.Supp 37 (D. Mass. 1990)
Microsoft	*Apple Computer, Inc. v. Microsoft Corporation and Hewlett-Packard Co.,* 35 F.3d 1435 (1994)
MTI/CAMS	*Manufacturers Technologies, Inc. v. CAMS, Inc.,* 706 F. Supp. 984 (D. Conn. 1989)
Nichols	*Nichols v. Universal Pictures Corp.,* 45 F.2d 119 (2d Cir.), Cert denied, 282 U.S. 902 (1930)
Peak	*MAI Systems Corp. v. Peak Computer, Inc.,* 991 F.2d 511 (9th Cir. 1993)
Pennwalt	*Pennwalt Corp. v. Durand-Wayland, Inc.,* 833 F.2d 931 (Fed. Cir. 1987)
Roth	*Roth Greeting Cards v. United Card Co.,* 429 F.2d 1106 (9th Cir. 1970)

SAS Institute	*SAS Institute, Inc. v. S & H Computer Systems, Inc.*, 605 F. Supp. 816 (M. D. Tenn., 1985)
Sega	*Sega Enterprises Ltd. v. Accolade, Inc.*, 977 F.2d 1510 (9th Cir. 1992)
Sid & Marty Krofft	*Sid & Marty Krofft Television Prod., Inc. v. McDonald's Corp.*, 562 F.2d 1157 (9th Cir. 1977)
Synercom	*Synercom Technology, Inc. v. University Computing Co.*, 462 F. Supp. 1003 (N. D. Texas, 1978)
Whelan	*Whelan Assoc. v. Jaslow Dental Laboratory, Inc.*, 797 F.2d 1222 (3rd Cir. 1986), cert denied, 479 U.S. 1031 (1987)
Williams	*Williams Electronics, Inc. v. Artic Int'l, Inc.*, 685 F.2d 870 (3rd Cir. 1982)

Recommended Reading

Brooks, F. P., Jr. *The Mythical Man-Month* (Reading, Mass.: Addison Wesley, 1975).

Clapes, A. L., P. Lynch, and M. R. Steinberg. "Silicon Epics and Binary Bards: Determining the Proper Scope of Copyright Protection for Computer Programs," *UCLA Law Review* 34(5 & 6) (1987): 1493–1594.

Clapes, A. *Software, Copyright, & Competition: The "Look and Feel" of the Law* (Westport, Conn.: Quorum Books, 1989).

Clapes, A. *Softwars: The Legal Battles for Control of the Global Software Industry* (Westport, Conn.: Quorum Books, 1993).

Lauckner, K. F. and R. C. Vile, Jr. *Computers: Inside & Out* (Ann Arbor, Mich.: Pippin Publishing, 1988).

Miller, Arthur R. "Copyright Protection for Computer Programs, Databases, and Computer-Generated Works: Is Anything New Since CONTU?" *Harvard Law Review* 106 (March 1993): 977–1073.

Paltry, William. *The Fair Use Privilege in Copyright Law* (Washington, D.C.: Bureau of National Affairs, 1985).

Patterson, L. R. and S. W. Lindberg. *The Nature of Copyright: A Law of Users' Rights* (Athens: University of Georgia Press, 1991).

Sammet, J. E. *Programming Languages: History and Fundamentals* (Englewood Cliffs, N.J.: Prentice-Hall, 1969).

U. S. Congress, Office of Technology Assessment, *Finding a Balance: Computer Software, Intellectual Property, and the Challenge of Technological Change*, OTA-TCT-527 (Washington, DC: U.S. Government Printing Office, 1992).

Index

Note: Bold face page numbers indicate the location of individual case discussions.

Abstraction, level of, 21, 86, 87

Abstraction-comparison-filtration (ACF) test, 86

Abstraction-filtration-comparison (AFC) test, 85, 86

Abstractions test. *See* Hand, Learned

Access, 70, 71, 76 n.3, 119, 125, 126

Accolade, Inc., 114–16

Address, 146

Advanced Micro Devices, Inc., 108

Advanced Software, Inc., 36, 38, 43

Algorithm, 30, 136, 164

Allen-Myland, Inc. (AMI), 57, 59

Allen-Myland, Inc. v. *IBM*, 57, **57**, 61

American National Standards Institute (ANSI), 75

American Standard Code for Information Interchange (ASCII), 145, 146

Analytic Dissection, 83–85, 87, 89 nn.4, 6

Antitrust law, 25

Appeals Court, 69

Apple Computer, Inc., 76 n.6, 84, 89 n.5

Apple Computer, Inc. v. *Formula Int'l*, **50**, 53 n.2, 163

Apple Computer, Inc. v. *Franklin Computer Corp.*, **52**, 52, 53 n.2

Apple Computer, Inc. v. *Microsoft*

Corporation and Hewlett-Packard Co., 75, **75**, 76 n.6, 84, 84, 91, 168

Application program, 50, 60, 101, 120, 162, 164, 174

Architectural works, 56

Architecture, 22, 25, 26, 121, 129, 143

Arithmetic/Logic unit (ALU), 146, 149, 150, 153, 172, 174

Arnstein v. *Porter*, 81, **82**, 82, 83

Arrangement, 63, 64

Ashton-Tate, Inc., 103

Assembler language, 106, 153, 187

Atanasoff, John V., 34, 35

Atari Games Corp. v. *Nintendo of America, Inc.*, 103, 111, **111**, 112, 113

Atari Games Corporation, 111, 113

AT&T Bell Telephone Laboratories, 103

Audiovisual works, 47, 48, 56

Authorship, 56, 64, 72

Baker v. *Selden*, 12, **13**, 16

Basic Input/Output system (BIOS), 131

Berne Copyright Convention, 56, 136

Bootstrapping, 142

Borland, Inc., 100

Bricklin, Dan, 30, 104 n.5

Britain, 2

Broderbund Software, Inc. v. *Unison World, Inc.*, **23**, 68, 80, 84

Brooks, Frederick P., Jr., 122 n.13

Brooktree Corp. v. *Advanced Micro Devices, Inc.*, 108, **108**

Business decision, 27, 115

Byte, 146

Central processing unit (CPU), 38, 60, 146, 180

Characters, 144, 146

Choices, 21, 25, 69, 78, 79, 88, 93, 119, 150, 166, 168, 170, 172, 174, 176

Choreographic works, 56

Claims, patent, 30, 40, 42, 188

Clapes, Anthony, 81, 89 n.2

Clean room, 27, 70, 71, 76 n.3, 125, 127, 129, 130

COMIT, 103

Communication, 47, 50

Compatibility, 97, 98, 117, 118

Compilation, 18, 61–63, 153

Compton Encyclopedia, Inc., 33, 34, 45 n.4, 137

Computer Associates Int'l, Inc. v. *Altai, Inc.*, 26, **27**, 71, 84, 85, 87, 88, 133

Computer program, 51, 149

Constitution, U. S., 3, 43

Control unit, 146, 149, 173, 174

Copy, archival, 59

Copying, 60

Copyright Act of 1976, 3, 4, 12, 19, 25, 29, 47, 51, 56, 57, 64, 67, 80, 102, 107, 112, 113, 115–17, 159

Copyright Act of 1980, 3, 29, 59, 102

Copyright Office, 55, 65 n.1, 73, 102, 107, 111, 122 n.6

Copyright law, 30, 108, 112, 133

Cursor, 38

Damages, 65 n.1, 72, 81

Data, 141

Database, software, 32

Davis, Randall, 87, 88

Decompilation, 122 n.2

Derivative work, 109, 158

Design, of a program, 80

Diamond, Commissioner of Patents and Trademarks v. *Diehr*, 30, **30**

Directive, Council of the European Community (CEC), 105, 110, 122 n.1

Disassembly, 105, 106, 108, 110, 113, 115–18, 121, 122 n.2

Dissection, 83–85, 87, 89 nn.4, 6

District Court, 69

Donaldson. *See In Re Donaldson Company, Inc.*

Dramatic works, 56

Eckert, J. Presper, 34, 35

Economists, 72

Efficiency, 26

Encyclopedia Brittanica, 45 n.4

ENIAC, 34. *See also Honeywell, Inc.* v. *Sperry Rand Corp. et al.*

Equivalents, 39, 40

Excel spreadsheet program, 98, 104 n.2

Expert testimony, 21, 72, 82, 83, 89 n.4, 100

Expression, 30, 56, 65, 72, 73, 82–84, 91, 99, 112, 116, 125, 128

Extrinsic test, 82

Fair use, 111–15, 117

Feist Publications, Inc., 62–64, 76 n.2

Feist Publications, Inc. v. *Rural Telephone Service Co., Inc.*, **62**

Finder, Macintosh, 76

Fixation, 47–49, 52, 60, 61

FORTRAN, 153, 155, 159, 165, 177 nn.7, 11

Fox Software, Inc., 103

Frybarger v. *International Business Machines Corporation*, 73, **74**

Fulton, Dave, 103

Gates Rubber Co. v. *Bando American, Inc.*, 85, **85**

Graphic, 56, 167, 168

Halliburton Oil Well Cementing Co. v. *C. P. Walker*, 40, **41**

Hardware, 56, 142, 143, 165

Harmonization, 136

Hashing, 38, 43, 45 n.7, 180, 183

Hewlett-Packard, Inc., 75, 76 n.6

Hiding, Principle of, 118, 121, 122 n.12
High-level language. *See* Language, high-level
Honeywell, Inc. v. *Sperry Rand Corp.*, 34, **35**

IBM Corporation, 57, 59, 61, 73, 101, 102, 130
Idea, 16, 22, 23, 30, 37, 56, 65, 72, 73, 80, 82–84, 99, 105, 125, 128
Idea/expression dichotomy, 11, 16, 21, 22, 24, 73, 80, 133, 136
In re Donaldson Company, Inc., 43, **44**
In re Alappat, **135**
Infoworld, 38, 104 n.6
Infringement, 65, 65 n.1, 67, 71, 72, 115, 125, 159
Input, 18, 141, 142, 161, 166
Instruction format, 151, 152
Instructions, 141, 142, 148, 151
Intellectual property, 102, 104, 135
Interface, 80, 84, 99, 119
Interoperability, 110, 117, 118, 121
Interpreter, 98, 158, 170, 173, 175
Interrupt, 38, 43, 45 n.7, 180
Intrinsic test, 82, 84
Inverse Ratio rule, 71
Iowa State University, 34, 35

Jeweler's Circular Publ. Co. v. *Keystone Publ. Co.*, 65 n.7

Keeton, Robert, 99, 100

Language, high-level, 8, 78, 101, 118, 122 n.2, 148, 153, 163, 164
Law of Nature, 134, 193
Hand, Learned, 20
Leasing companies, 58
Lehman, Bruce, 33
Library of Congress, 55
License, software, 32, 60
Life cycle, software, 118, 122 n.13
Lisa, 75, 84, 89 n.5
Literary works, 47, 56, 59, 73
Location, in memory, 146
Look and feel, 91
Lotus 1-2-3 spreadsheet program, 91, 92, 96, 98–100, 104 n.1
Lotus Development Corp., 101
Lotus Development Corp. v. *Borland International, Inc.*, **100**, 100, 103
Lotus Development Corp. v. *Paperback Software Int'l*, 80, 91, **91**, 92, 97, 100–103, 104 n.4, 168

Macintosh, 75, 84, 89 n.5
Macro, 88, 96, 97, 99, 100, 168, 170, 177 n.10
MAI Systems Corp. v. *Peak Computer, Inc.*, 60, **61**
MAI Systems Corporation, 60
Manufacturers Technologies, Inc. v. *CAMS, Inc.*, 16, **17**, 19
Marker, copyright, 22, 55, 56, 167
Mask work, 107, 109, 122 n.4
Mathematical algorithm, 30, 31, 45 n.3, 134, 191
Mauchly, John, 34, 35
Means-plus-function, 40, 42, 43
Medium, 141
Medium, tangible, 47–49
Memory, 26, 143, 146, 149, 150, 173
Menu tree, 92, 93, 96–100
Merger, 23–25, 56, 65, 72–74, 77, 99, 116, 128
Method, 13, 38, 40
Microcode, 8, 22, 25, 26, 53, 56, 72, 168, 172
Microinstructions, 175
Microsoft, Inc., 75, 84, 98
Monitor, clean-room, 127, 129, 131 n.4
Mosaic Software, Inc., 104 n.4
Motion pictures, 47, 56
Multi-media, 33, 45 n.5
Musical works, 56

NEC, Inc. v. *Intel, Inc.*, **22**, 25, 53, 55, 73, 76 nn.4, 5
National Commission on New Technological Uses of Copyrighted Works, 29, 51, 67, 102
Nichols v. *Universal Pictures Corp.*, 20, **20**
Nintendo of America, Inc., 111, 113
Non-literal elements, 15, 91

Notice, copyright, 22, 55, 56, 167
Novel, 12, 30, 31, 37, 192
New York Times, 31

Object code, 48–52, 115, 153, 155, 163
Obvious, 12, 30, 31, 37
Operating system, 8, 50, 52, 60, 101, 102,
    115, 120, 131, 162–65
Ordinary observer, 80, 83, 84
Organization, 88
Original work, 64, 72
Output, 141, 143, 161

Pantomimes, 56
Paper trail, 108, 109, 127
Paperback Software, Inc., 98, 99
Parameters, 88, 168, 170, 171, 177 n.10
Parnas, David L., 122 n.12
Pascal, 159, 163, 177 n.7, 187
Patent Act of 1952, 40
Patent Law Reform, Advisory
    Commission on, 134, 136
Patent law, 30, 108, 142
Peak Computer, Inc., 60
Pennsylvania, University of, 34, 35
Pennwalt Corp. v. *Durand-Wayland,
    Inc.*, 41, **42**
Perlis, Alan J., 104
Personal computer (PC), 130
Phoenix Technologies, Inc,, 130
Pictorial, 56
Piracy, 67
Pre-existing material, 61, 63
Preferred embodiment, 38, 39
Prior art, 32, 33, 36, 39
Process, 31
Program, application.   Application
    program
Program, computer, 51, 149
Protection, copyright, 11, 28 n.1, 48, 63,
    103, 141, 167
Protection, intellectual property, 110,
    137, 165, 176
Protection, patent, 11, 31, 38, 103
Publici juris, 65 n.8

Quattro Pro spreadsheet program, 100,
    104 n.2

Queen, Cary L., 36

Random access memory (RAM), 8, 60,
    146
Re-examination, 32, 33
Read-only memory (ROM), 8, 50, 52,
    146
Registers, 146
Registration, copyright, 55, 65 n.1, 73
Remington Rand Corporation, 34
Results, 141
Reverse engineering, 105–15, 121
Roth Greeting Cards v. *United Card Co.*,
    70, **70**, 79
Rubber-curing process, 31
Rule of thumb, 118, 122 n.13
Rural Telephone Service Co., Inc.,
    62–64, 76 n.2

Santa Cruz Operation (SCO), 100
SAS Institute, Inc. v. *S & H Computer
    Systems, Inc.*, **14**, 15, 68, 79, 80
Scenes a faire, 74, 84
Scope, of copyright, 48, 63, 92, 101
Screen presentation, 17, 77, 84, 167
Sculptural works, 56
Searches, 33
Sega Enterprises Ltd. v. *Accolade, Inc.*,
    103, 111, **114**, 117
Sega Enterprises, Ltd., 114, 115
Selection, 63, 64
Semiconductor Chip Protection Act of
    1984 (SCPA), 107, 110
Sequence, 18, 19, 88
Sequential storage, 177 n.2
Sequential memory, 177 n.2
SHARE, 101, 102
Sid & Marty Krofft Television Prod., Inc.
    v. *McDonald's Corp.*, 71, **82**, 82–84
Similarity, 69, 71, 83, 107
Similarity, substantial, 70–72, 77, 80–85,
    119, 159
Skilled in the art, 30, 35
Smoking gun, 69
SNOBOL, 103
Software, 146
Software Patent Institute (SPI), 33, 35,
    36, 133, 134

Software industry, 8, 9, 101, 102, 119, 167, 176
Sound recordings, 56
Source code, 15, 48, 49, 51, 77, 88, 111, 131
Sperry Rand Corporation, 34
Spreadsheet, 30, 92, 93, 96, 98, 104 n.1
Squibb Corporation. v. *Diagnostic Medical Instruments, Inc.*, 122 n.5
Standard, 74, 75, 84, 104, 136, 155
Stephenson, James, 96
Storage, 26, 143, 146, 149, 150, 173
Structure, 42, 88; dynamic, 87, 89 n.8; static, 87, 89 n.8
Structure, sequence, and organization, 14, 15, 80, 87, 88, 131 n.3, 133
Sub-routine, 87, 88, 89 n.7, 162, 170–72
Supreme Court, 29–31, 40, 41, 45 n.3, 69, 192, 194
Sweat of the brow, 63, 64
Synercom Technology, Inc., v. *University Computing Co.*, **18**, 28 n.2

Tangible medium, 47–49
Text processing, 37
Total concept and feel, 70, 79, 80, 84
Trade secret law, 2, 86, 109
Trade secrets, 106, 110
Translation, 97, 153, 155, 158, 163, 164
Trier of fact, 81, 83, 89 n.3

Two-step test, 83

Unbundling of software, 101, 102
U. S. Congress, 107
U. S. Patent & Trademark Office (PTO), 31–33, 35–38, 43, 102, 133, 137, 194
UNIX, 36
Useful, 12, 30, 99, 192
User interface, 77, 79, 84, 91, 101, 102, 131 n.3, 133, 165–68
Utilitarian, 8, 52, 99
Utility program, 162, 164

Validity, of copyright, 48
Venture capital, 32
Virtual identical copying, 48, 74
VisiCalc, 30, 96
VP-Planner, 96, 99, 104 n.2

Whelan Assoc. v. *Jaslow Dental Laboratory, Inc.*, 4, 13, **14**, 19, 23, 79, 80, 83, 87, 88, 133
White-Smith Music Publishing Co. v. *Apollo Co.*, 53 n.1
Williams Electronics, Inc. v. *Artic Int'l, Inc.*, 47, **48**, 52, 67
Windows, 75
Word processing, 37
Work for hire, 28 n.1

ABOUT THE AUTHOR

BERNARD A. GALLER is Professor Emeritus, University of Michigan, and has served as an expert witness in major intellectual property cases during the last 15 years. He is founder and president of the Software Patent Institute, founding editor-in-chief of the *Annals of the History of Computing*, and a former president of the Association for Computing Machinery. Among his books are *The Language of Computers* (1962) and *A View of Programming languages* (with A. J. Perlis, 1970).